COZY
HRISTMAS
ROCHET

Classic Scandinavian Projects
to Brighten Your Home

HANNESEN & PIA H. H. JOHANNESEN

SCHIFFER CRAFT
4880 Lower Valley Road • Atglen, PA 19310

Other Schiffer Craft Books on Related Subjects:

Knitting for Little Sweethearts,
ISBN 978-0-7643-5627-8

All-Year-Round Knitting for Little Sweethearts: 68 Patterns for Everyday, Parties, and Special Times,
ISBN 978-0-7643-6507-2

Summer Knitting for Little Sweethearts, 40 Nordic-Style Warm Weather Patterns for Girls, Boys, and Babies,
ISBN 978-0-7643-6606-2

Winter Knitting for Little Sweethearts: 46 Nordic-Style Patterns for Girls, Boys, and Babies,
ISBN 978-0-7643-6844-8

Originally published as *Haeklet klassisk julepynt 2* by Heidi B. Johannesen and Pia H. H. Johannesen, © 2024 by Turbine Forlaget

Translated from the Norwegian by Carol Huebescher Rhoades

Library of Congress Control Number: 2026933178

Designed by Karin Hald
Front cover design by Lindsay Hess
Photography by David Bering / Montgomery
Type set in BentonSans

ISBN: 978-0-7643-7248-3
ePub: 978-1-5073-0765-6

Printed in China

10 9 8 7 6 5 4 3 2 1

FSC www.fsc.org MIX Paper | Supporting responsible forestry FSC® C104723

Published by Schiffer Craft
An imprint of Schiffer Publishing, Ltd.
4880 Lower Valley Road
Atglen, PA 19310
Phone: (610) 593-1777; Fax: (610) 593-2002
Email: Info@schifferbooks.com
Web: www.schifferbooks.com

For our complete selection of fine books on this and related subjects, please visit our website at www.schifferbooks.com. You may also write for a free catalog.

Schiffer Publishing's titles are available at special discounts for bulk purchases for sales promotions or premiums. Special editions, including personalized covers, corporate imprints, and excerpts, can be created in large quantities for special needs. For more information, contact the publisher.

We are always looking for people to write books on new and related subjects. If you have an idea for a book, please contact us at proposals@schifferbooks.com.

CONTENTS

PREFACE

Cozy Christmas Crochet is the third book we've published of our crocheted Christmas decorations. The first book featured bright colors and Nordic simplicity. The next book was filled with traditional and classic Christmas decorations in shades of red.

We've had at the very *least* one more book's worth of creative, classic Christmas decoration designs in our heads, so this book is a completely natural extension of our other book of classic decorations. We are so proud and happy to offer you ten new patterns. We're also happy that these new crocheted ornaments decorated our own Christmas homes this year as well as our shop in Haslev, Denmark.

You'll find crocheted ornaments in red, white, and green combined with a fair amount of gold and glitter. Many people connect these colors with traditional Christmas decorations and remember them from their own childhoods. We've also noted that traditional decorations have a bigger and bigger place in homes at Christmas every year, creating memories and nostalgia. Our new crochet designs for Christmas decorations are carefully chosen to fit in with our existing treasured ornament collections and the style of our homes.

Have we finished developing crocheted Christmas decorations with this book? No, we can say with certainty. We love everything associated with Christmas and we love to design crocheted Christmas decorations. There are still many Christmas ornaments to be designed!

We hope that, with the patterns in this book, you'll enjoy crocheting Christmas decorations . . . and that the decorations you make will have a special meaning for you or whoever you make them for.

You'll find patterns for a sweet little gingerbread house and gingerbread hearts, the most outstanding nutcracker, pretty bows, drums with space for surprises, striped ornaments, gift bags that can also be used as Advent bags, tiny stockings, mushrooms, and even some mini mistletoe.

We wish you immense pleasure as you crochet these Christmas decorations.

Merry Christmas!
Heidi and Pia

ABOUT THIS BOOK

In this book, you'll find ten patterns for crocheted classic Christmas decorations. Many of the patterns include several variations and sizes, so there are plenty of options for crocheting different Christmas decorations.

There are patterns for new crocheters as well as for those who are more experienced. There are large and small projects, quick and more time-consuming projects. Everyone can come along in this book and, if you come across techniques you aren't familiar with, you shouldn't worry. We've included lots of help, including with many video clips made especially for these projects.

Under each basic pattern, you'll find a list of the materials and tools you'll need, what crochet gauge to start from, as well as measurements for the finished item. You'll also find a short section with tips for getting good results for the basic pattern, as well as an explanation of the skill level.

Some patterns include charts and drawings in addition to the written text, as a good supplement to the project.

The section "General Instructions" in the basic patterns succinctly describes the process of working through the design. This section includes important information that you need to be aware of. Before you begin to crochet, be sure to carefully read all through the pattern so you won't miss any important information.

Some patterns are accompanied by charts and illustrations to further explain the written text and serve as good supplements to the text.

VIDEO GUIDES AND HELP

For each pattern, you'll find a QR code linked to a playlist on YouTube, where we've collected all the relevant video guides with techniques and assembly for each single pattern.

Most iPhones and Android phones have a camera that will scan a QR code. QR codes link you to a playlist on YouTube with the video guides for that pattern. On some phones, it is necessary to first download a QR code scanner.

How to Scan the QR Codes

- Open the camera on your phone.
- Hold your phone so the camera viewfinder focuses on the QR code.
- The phone should recognize the QR code and you'll get a notification.
- Press the notification and you'll be taken to the link for the QR code.

When the playlist opens, YouTube will automatically play the first video of the playlist. Or you can scroll through the playlist and choose the video you want to watch.

You can also go directly to our YouTube channel, www.youtube.com/kreadeluxe, and find our playlists and the videos for each of the patterns.

SKILL LEVELS

Each of the patterns in the book is marked with one of three skill levels: beginner, intermediate, and experienced.

Each pattern begins with a short description, so you'll know why the design is listed at a specified skill level. Even if you think the pattern might be a bit hard for you, you shouldn't let yourself be limited by the skill level designations. There are plenty of good video clips for each pattern that can help you understand anything, including finishing, that you aren't sure of and for anything you might not have tried previously.

Simple patterns for those who are inexperienced but familiar with the basic crochet stitches. If you are beginning to crochet or haven't crocheted from crochet patterns before, we recommend that you begin with patterns at this skill level.

Most crocheters with some experience at reading patterns should have no trouble with these patterns.

Patterns for experienced crocheters who can work with more detailed designs. These are the patterns for anyone who likes challenges or those with more complex finishing.

YARN

We used the following yarns for the patterns in this book:

Organic Cotton, Organic Wool 1, Deluxe Silk Mohair, and Shiny Glimmergarn, all from Krea Deluxe.

These yarns are produced with an uncompromising commitment to sustainability, with the greatest consideration for the environment, people, and animals. Organic Cotton and Organic Wool 1 are also GOTS-certified under Krea Deluxe's license number 1117459.

Of course, you can use other yarns—it is important, though, that the crochet hook size and the yarn suit each other. Also make sure that the yarn is the same size (yards/meters per ounces/grams) so the finished product will be the same size and measurements as given in the book.

Organic Cotton
GOTS-certified organic cotton yarn (100% cotton, 180 yd/165 m / 50 g, CYCA 2, sport)

Organic Wool 1
GOTS-certified organic wool yarn (100% wool, 164 yd/150 m / 50 g, CYCA 2, sport)

Deluxe Silk Mohair
(45% silk, 33% mohair, 22% baby alpaca, 262 yd/240 m / 20 g, CYCA 1, lace)

Shiny Glimmergarn
(80% rayon/viscose, 20% polyester, 104 yd/95 m / 25 g, CYCA 1, fingering)

Krea Deluxe
ORGANIC WOOL

FIBERFILL

We used kapok as the fiberfill for all the projects in this book. Kapok is an organic natural fiber that is both hypoallergenic and antibacterial. Kapok is derived from seed capsules of the tall kapok trees (*Ceiba pentranda*). Kapok trees grow wild in the tropical rainforests of India, South and Central America, and in western Africa on plantations in the wild rainforest. They can grow naturally there under the same conditions as for the rest of the rainforest.

Kapok consists of a naturally bitter substance, which means that the kapok trees are not attacked by pests. For that reason, it is not necessary to use chemicals, pesticides, or other sprays during cultivation, harvesting, or production of kapok. The bitter substance gives the fiber the fantastic advantage that mold and house dust mites cannot live in the fiber, and it also means that kapok fiberfill is a hypoallergenic and hygienic product that lasts for many years.

Kapok fiber contains 80% air and is eight times lighter than cotton. It is a light material that you can enjoy because it takes fewer grams of kapok than other fiberfills for a project. It takes between half and two-thirds the amount of kapok relative to other fillers. This also depends on the item and how firm or soft you want your finished product to be. Kapok is easy to make compact and firm, and, for all these reasons, it is our choice for filling our crocheted Christmas decorations.

We prefer using kapok because it is easy to work with, but, of course, you can use the type of fiberfill you prefer.

FILLED LIKE A BALLOON

For a uniform filling without any lumps, you can try our simple "balloon tip."

- Begin by filling out the sides of the item so it almost makes a padding on the inside of the figure.
- Next, fill in the middle. This way, the figure will be filled from the center out—somewhat like blowing air into a balloon.
- Use a lot of filling. The item is filled when the figure's holds its shape. It should be filled well enough so the figure won't lose its silhouette when you press on it.
- Filling often compresses with use, so, it is good to add a bit extra filling to prevent the figure from becoming slack or to shrink together.

TOOLS

When you are undertaking a large production of crocheted Christmas decorations, some tools will make the job so much easier. Here are our best tips for the necessary tools.

Crochet Hooks
The type of crochet hook you use can make a great difference in your results and the pleasure gained from crochet. It is the most important tool and should be chosen so that the work glides smoothly without any problems, so you can relax your hand and arm muscles as you crochet. The crochet hook should have a sharp hook and a relatively short neck so it will be easy to insert into the stitch loops and easy to catch the yarn.

Most important of all, the hook should fit well in your hand, not slide around, and it should be comfortable to work with. This will help you achieve good results, rather than counterbalancing your work. We usually compare it to a carpenter not wanting to cut with a dull saw.

We swear by the Clover Soft Touch or Clover Amour hooks, both excellent brands of hook. We regularly alternate between the two types because they are shaped differently and have different handles. It will be good for your hands if you change between these two types of hook when you are crocheting for many hours.

Measuring Tape and Gauge Measure
A gauge measure is usually used to measure knitting gauge but it can also be used for crochet projects. The placed square makes it easy to measure the number of stitches over 4" × 4" (10 × 10 cm) when you crochet back and forth in rows. If you don't have a gauge measure, you can use a regular ruler instead. A flexible measuring tape is a necessary tool for measuring the crochet gauge of round figures and shapes.

Small Pointed Scissors
It's helpful to have pointed scissors near at hand for trimming ends and for opening up seams. The classic stork scissors will fit well in your hand and be stable when the scissor bow is placed over the index finger of the hand you hold your scissors in.

Needles

Needles of various sizes, with pointed or blunt tips, can make a big difference and lighten the work when finishing. A curved needle is the most ingenious needle invented for this purpose. It moves smoothly in and out of a figure, which can be difficult with a regular straight needle. A long, thin doll needle can also be a big help when you are sewing through a figure or have tight stitches and you have use for something to hold it in. A sharp tip needle is also good to have when making holes, while a blunt tip needle is good for existing holes as, for example, when weaving in ends and embroidering cross stitch. Don't forget that the needle should suit the yarn and the crocheted piece because it is not easy to insert a large tapestry needle through tiny stitches.

Stitch Markers and Marking Thread

It is advantageous to have a stitch marker or marking thread to indicate where the beginning and end is when crocheting around in rounds. If you don't use some type of marker, it will be easy to lose your place because, after a couple of rounds, it will be difficult to see where the round begins or ends.

Locking ring (moveable) stitch markers are especially good to use when you have long rounds and want to avoid having to count repeatedly. Before the round begins, you can count out the stitches and place a marker in the stitches where increases and decreases will be made. That way, you avoid having to count if your thoughts wander to something else while you crochet.

A Knitting Needle or Pencil

A knitting needle or the end of a pencil without an eraser is your best friend for poking filling into smaller areas.

Krea Deluxe

CROCHET GAUGE
Is It Really So Important?

Even if you have crocheted many projects previously, we strongly recommend that you read through this section before you begin any of the patterns. Crochet gauge is absolutely crucial for the final results when making the small decorative objects in this book.

The crochet gauge, which we list in each pattern, refers to how tightly the crochet work should be in the stitch structure so you will obtain the same look and size as the pieces shown in the photos and as described in the pattern. You might also find that the gauge can be different in different patterns even when they use the same yarn.

If, for example, you crochet the nutcracker more loosely than at the recommended gauge, he will be shaped differently and will have a sloppy structure, making it difficult to assemble him correctly. If you crochet the pieces for the drums too loosely or too tightly, you risk having pieces that won't fit together with the cardstock inner drum when you assemble the parts.

Crochet gauge is also important for the yarn amount you use. If you crochet more loosely than recommended in the pattern, you will need to use more yarn and, if you originally purchased only the recommended amount, you may need to buy more yarn for your project.

We always recommend that you crochet a gauge swatch before you begin a project. It will help you be certain that the yarn and hook suit each other and that you'll achieve the gauge given in the pattern.

Important Note: The size for the crochet hook given in the pattern is always just a recommendation. For that reason, it is always a good idea to make a crocheted gauge swatch to be sure that your hook size is the best one for you to achieve the given gauge.

Technique Videos for Gauge

These are the techniques: A crocheted swatch worked back and forth in rows, a crocheted swatch worked around in rounds.

Make a Gauge Swatch

To make a gauge swatch, you should crochet a piece measuring at least 4" × 4" (10 × 10 cm). The stitches around the edges, top and bottom of a swatch will have a different gauge than the stitches in the middle of the swatch. So, really, the swatch should be larger than 4" × 4" (10 × 10 cm). You can do this by chaining one and a half times as many stitches as given for the pattern's gauge. That way, you should end up with a swatch about 6" (15 cm) in width.

For example:
For a gauge of 30 stitches: multiply the stitch count of 30 times 1.5—30 × 1.5 = 45.

Begin by chaining 45 stitches for a crochet gauge swatch.

Use the hook size recommended for the gauge for your first swatch and then adjust it if necessary.

For a swatch worked back and forth in rows:

- Chain the needed number of stitches with the hook size recommended for the gauge in the pattern.
- Work rows back and forth in single crochet until the piece is 6" (15 cm) high.
- Lay your swatch on a flat surface—avoid stretching or pulling it out of shape.
- Place a gauge measure or straight ruler over the gauge swatch to measure the center stitches.
- Count the number of stitches in 4" (10 cm) across the width and the number of rows in 4" (10 cm) of the length.
- If your swatch does not match the given crochet gauge in the pattern, follow the advice on page 21.

For a swatch worked around in rounds:

- Chain the needed number of stitches with the hook size recommended for the gauge in the pattern.
- Join the chain into a ring and work around in single crochet until the piece is 6" (15cm) high.
- Place a measuring tape on the gauge swatch along one of the rounds.
- Insert a pin at each end of a 4" (10 cm) section.
- Count the number of stitches in 4" (10 cm) of the width and number of rows in 4" (10cm) of the length.
- If your swatch does not match the given crochet gauge in the pattern, follow the advice on page 21.

Your swatch has fewer stitches than given in the pattern gauge

If you have a tendency to crochet loosely, you will have fewer stitches and rows/rounds over 4" × 4" (10 × 10 cm) than given in the pattern. Your work will be sloppy and the stitch structure will be so loose that the filling will be visible through the stitches.

You can adjust your gauge by doing the following:

- Use a smaller size crochet hook.
- Make sure that the loops on the hook are close enough so they don't gape when you bring the yarn through them. If, at the same time, you tighten up the yarn from the hook to the opposite hand, the stitch structure will automatically become tighter. The size of the hook neck determines the size of the crocheted stitches. You can control this by making sure that the loops on the hook are close together on the hook so the stitches don't gape when the yarn comes through them. In addition, the yarn between the hook and your hand, where the yarn sits, should be taut. This way, you will automatically make the crochet work firm and tight enough in the stitch structure so that you can achieve the gauge given in the pattern.

Your swatch has more stitches than given in the pattern gauge

If you have a tendency to crochet tightly, you will have more stitches and rows/rounds over 4" × 4" (10 × 10 cm) than given in the pattern. This will affect the project's finished measurements, which will be smaller than those given.

Your work will be stiff and the stitch structure will be so tight that it will be difficult to insert the hook through the stitch loops.

You can adjust your gauge by doing the following:

- Use a larger size crochet hook.
- Loosen the yarn on the finger where your yarn sits. Angle your index finger a bit forward so you can loosen the yarn and also the work.

MULTICOLOR CROCHET

Some of the patterns in this book are crocheted with various patterns and stripes. You'll find different techniques for multicolor crochet, and, in this book, we used both Gobelin and jacquard crochet.

For both techniques, it is important that the yarn not be tightened too much because that will make the pattern pull in. Stretch the work out after every row to make sure that the stitch structure hasn't become uneven and tight.

Jacquard Crochet
Jacquard crochet involves working a pattern with two or more colors at a time. The color not in use hangs on the wrong side of the work and is picked up when needed again. The strands on the wrong side are called floats. The floats should be precisely as long as necessary so the stitches don't pull in because they are too tight, or, on the other hand, hang too loosely and make the stitches too loose.

Make sure that the floats are placed on the wrong side so they won't lie on the right side of the work and be visible on the finished Christmas decoration. On the rows where several color changes occur on the row, you can make small bundles ("butterflies") of yarn that hang on the wrong side and are picked up as needed. This way, you won't have long threads hanging down and crossing on large areas of the work.

Gobelin Crochet
By using the Gobelin crochet technique, you can make the most beautiful color patterns that look the same on both right and wrong sides.

This technique creates a very stable and strong stitch structure when crocheted around over the color not in use. This way, the color not in use goes all around the work without hanging as floats on the wrong side.

Changing Colors
To change colors neatly, change to the new color before you work the last step of the last stitch before the color change.

Technique Videos for Multicolor Crochet
These are the techniques: Gobelin crochet, Jacquard crochet, color changes, sharp color transition when crocheting around in a spiral.

FINISHING AND BLOCKING

You will produce a really nice and uniform result in your finished project if you block all the pieces separately before you join them. Only flat pieces are blocked. Crocheted pieces with a more three-dimensional form, such as Christmas balls and the nutcracker are not blocked.

Blocking a finished piece means stretching and forming it to the right shape, which also smooths out and straightens the stitches. When wet-blocking, the pieces should stay in the position they are laid out in until they are completely dry and, that way, are forced into a completely controlled shape. This creates a very nice result and a knife-sharp finish.

How to Block:

- Wet the pieces by washing them in a bowl of water or spraying them with a water sprayer.
- Press and squeeze the water out. Avoid wringing because you might wring the pieces out of shape and distort the fibers in the yarn. You can also squeeze out any remaining water out by laying the pieces between two towels and rolling and pressing the towels.
- Lay the crocheted pieces, unfolded, on a plate covered with a hand towel.
- You can, for example, use a Styrofoam plate or cork bulletin board. If you don't have that, lay the pieces on a hand towel. Stretch the pieces out and shape them before pinning into place. Set pins into each of the small important details so they stay firmly in place. The more thoroughly you shape the pieces, the nicer the results.
- Leave the pieces pinned in place until they are completely dry.
- Additionally, you can steam press the pieces on the wrong side to iron out any remaining unevenness. Avoid ironing back and forth to prevent stretching the pieces out of shape. Be extra careful that you don't iron the stitches flat on both sides of the work.

ABBREVIATIONS AND TECHNIQUES

BL	back loop
ch	chain stitch
ch lp	chain loop
cm	centimeter(s)
dc	double crochet (= British treble crochet)
dec	decrease
esc	elongated single-crochet stitch (esc) is worked as for a normal single crochet, but, instead of inserting the hook under the top loop(s) of the stitch in the previous row, it is inserted into the base of that single crochet.
FL	front loop
fp-hdc	front post half double crochet = yarn over hook as for half double crochet, insert hook from right front to back of stitch post in row below and out at left front, yarn over hook and complete hdc as usual
hdc	half double crochet (= British half treble crochet)
in	inch(es)
inc	increase
lp	loop = strand on back of a chain stitch
m	meters
mm	millimeters
rnd(s)	round(s)
RS	right side
sc	single crochet (= British double crochet)
sk-dec	skip decrease = decrease 1 st by skipping a stitch
sl	slip
st(s)	stitch(es)
tc	turning chain
tog	together
tr	treble crochet (= British double treble)
WS	wrong side
yd	yard(s)
yoh	yarn over hook

Magic Ring

A magic ring is useful for beginning a small circular piece of crochet.

Make a loop (ring) with the yarn end to the left and on top of the working yarn. Insert the hook from the right side of the loop, under the yarn and then left, over the yarn. Catch working yarn over the hook and come back through the loop. Yarn around hook and through the loop on hook. Make sure you encase both strands of the ring as you work. Continue around as instructed in pattern. Later, you can pull the yarn end to tighten up and close the ring.

THE PROJECTS

CHRISTMAS ORNAMENTS

Christmas ornaments in spherical ball shapes or teardrop shapes are true classics for the Christmas tree. This crocheted version can be made in a range of colors so each will have a unique personality. With their curving shape and colorful stripes, they will embellish the Christmas tree alone or alongside some pretty glass balls. If you embroider the stripes with glitter yarn, they will have a more festive look and shine a little as they catch the rays from the Christmas lights.

Skill Level

These striped Christmas ornaments have several color changes on a single round. It takes a little practice to hold the yarn and crochet firmly and evenly at the same time as making the color changes. Don't give up on the first part of the piece even if it seems difficult. It gets easier as soon as your hands memorize the system of increases and decreases.

How to Achieve Good Results

The Christmas ornaments get their teardrop shape through increases and decreases. Fiberfill in the piece is used so the shape will come out correctly. For that reason, you must crochet very tightly and firmly, so the filling won't spill out between the stitches. As long as it is crocheted uniformly, evenly, and firmly, the ornament will almost shape itself. Weigh the given amount of fiberfill you use for each ornament to ensure that you have the right amount of fiberfill in each one. That way, it will be easier to shape the last section and achieve the given measurements with good results.

Technique Videos for Christmas Ornaments

These are the techniques: Chain stitch, slip stitch, single crochet stitch, magic ring, crocheting around in a spiral, increasing, decreasing, crocheting in back loop, jacquard crochet, changing colors, embroidering stripes, finishing the Christmas ornament.

MATERIALS

Yarn and Fiberfill

Organic Cotton
14 g for a single-color ornament or 7 g each of two colors for a striped ornament

Shiny Glimmergarn
4 g for top, stripes, and cord

OR

Shiny Glimmergarn
8 g for a single-color ornament or 4 g each of two colors for a striped ornament

4 g for top, stripes, and cord

8 g fiberfill for an ornament crocheted with Organic Cotton, 6 g for an ornament crocheted with Shiny Glimmergarn

Yarn Colors and Amounts
The ornaments shown were crocheted with colors 01, Natural White, 35 Red, 36 Army Green, as well as red and gold Glimmergarn

TOOLS

Recommended crochet hook: U.S. steel size 4 (2 mm) for Organic Cotton and U.S. size 4/0 (1.75 mm) for Shiny Glimmergarn

Notions: Blunt tapestry needle to weave in ends, scissors

Optional: a small curved needle for finishing

FINISHED MEASUREMENTS

Ornament crocheted with Organic Cotton:
Approx. 4¼" (11 cm) long and 2" (5 cm) in diameter

Ornament crocheted with Shiny Glimmergarn:
Approx. 4" (10 cm) long and 1¾" (4.5 cm) in diameter

Gauge

38 sts × 36 rnds crocheted around in jacquard technique with Organic Cotton and hook U.S. steel size 4 (2 mm) = 4" × 4" / 10 × 10 cm.

Adjust hook size to obtain correct gauge if necessary.

To achieve a tighter gauge with Shiny Glimmergarn, it is advantageous to use a smaller hook size, for example, U.S. steel size 5 (1.75 mm). We don't recommend using a smaller hook than that because the hook might be too small to catch the yarn.

Crochet Tips

If you want to skip making a gauge swatch, you can measure the width over three stripes on the first ornament you crochet. Two red and one white stripe should measure approx. 1⅜" (3.5 cm) with Organic Cotton. If you are working with Shiny Glimmergarn, it will be slightly smaller. If your ornament is wider, it means you are crocheting more loosely than specified in the patten.

VARIATIONS

The Christmas ornament can be worked in several different variations. In this pattern, the ornaments were crocheted with Organic Cotton or Shiny Glimmergarn. In addition, stripes were embroidered down each ornament.
The pattern is written with the starting point of a two-color variation. If you prefer a single-color version, you can work from the same pattern and just ignore the color changes.

VARIATION 1

This Christmas ornament is crocheted with two different colors of Organic Cotton with the top crocheted with Shiny Glimmergarn. If you want to further embellish your ornament, you can embroider the crocheted stripes with Shiny Glimmergarn.

VARIATION 2

This Christmas ornament is crocheted with one color of Organic Cotton while the top is crocheted with Shiny Glimmergarn. If you want to further embellish your ornament, you can embroider the crocheted stripes with Shiny Glimmergarn.

VARIATION 3

This Christmas ornament and top are crocheted with one color of Organic Cotton or Shiny Glimmergarn. If you want to further embellish your ornament, you can embroider the crocheted stripes with Shiny Glimmergarn as for Variations 1 and 2.

ORNAMENT CONSTRUCTION

The Christmas ornament is crocheted from the bottom up. Beginning on the 4th round, the color changes as you work up the rounds. The first color change round might be a bit tricky with so few stitches, but, it gets easier as the rounds gain more stitches.
The colors to crochet with are given as Color 1 and Color 2.
On rounds worked with two colors, Color 1 is coded with red and Color 2 with green. The color is listed before the stitches.

The 1st, 2nd, 3rd, and 40th, 41st, and 42nd rounds are crocheted exclusively with Color 1. All the other rounds are worked with two colors.
In this pattern, Color 1 is Red and Color 2 is White.
For example:
(Color 1 1 sc in next st, Color 2 1 sc in next st) 6 times.

Meaning: Crochet 1 sc in Color 1 followed by 1 sc in Color 2 and work that sequence a total of 6 times around.

When you are halfway through and, again, at the end, you can embroider the stripes on the Christmas ornament using back stitch.

The top and cord are crocheted separately and then sewn on later.

The piece is crocheted around in a spiral throughout. If necessary, use a marking thread or stitch marker to indicate the beginning and end of each round.

CHRISTMAS ORNAMENT

The first 3 rnds are worked only with Color 1.

Use crochet hook U.S. steel size 4 (2 mm) or size needed to obtain correct gauge.

Rnd 1: Work 6 sc around magic ring = 6 sts.

Rnd 2: (Inc, 1 sc in next st) 3 times = 9 sts.

Rnd 3: 1 sc in each st around = 9 sts.

From the next rnd through Rnd 39, work with 2 colors.

Rnd 4: (Color 1 1 sc in next st, in next st, work 1 sc each with Colors 2 and 1 [= 1 inc with both colors in same stx), 1 sc with Color 2 in next st] 3 times) = 12 sts.

Rnd 5: (Color 1 1 sc in next st, Color 2 1 sc in next st) 6 times = 12 sts.

Rnd 6: (Color 1 inc, Color 2 1 sc in next st) 6 times = 18 sts.

Rnd 7: (Color 1 1 sc in each of next 2 sts, Color 2 1 sc in next st) 6 times = 18 sts.

Rnd 8: (Color 1 1 sc in each of next 2 sts, Color 2 inc) 6 times = 24 sts.

Rnd 9: (Color 1 1 sc in each of next 2 sts, Color 2 1 sc in each of next 2 sts) 6 times = 24 sts.

Rnd 10: (Color 1 1 sc in next st, inc, Color 2 1 sc in each of next 2 sts) 6 times = 30 sts.

Rnd 11: (Color 1 1 sc in each of next 3 sts, Color 2 1 sc in each of next 2 sts) 6 times = 30 sts.

Rnd 12: (Color 1 1 sc in each of next 3 sts, Color 2 1 sc in next st, inc) 6 times = 36 sts.

Rnd 13: (Color 1 1 sc in each of next 3 sts, Color 2 1 sc in each of next 3 sts) 6 times = 36 sts.

Rnd 14: (Color 1 1 sc in each of next 2 sts, inc, Color 2 1 sc in each of next 3 sts) 6 times = 42 sts.

Rnd 15: (Color 1 1 sc in each of next 4 sts, Color 2 1 sc in each of next 3 sts) 6 times = 42 sts.

Rnd 16: (Color 1 1 sc in each of next 4 sts, Color 2 1 sc in each of next 2 sts, inc) 6 times = 48 sts.

Rnd 17: (Color 1 1 sc in each of next 3 sts, inc, Color 2 1 sc in each of next 4 sts) 6 times = 54 sts.

Rnds 18–26: (Color 1 1 sc in each of next 5 sts, inc, Color 2 1 sc in each of next 4 sts) 6 times = 54 sts.

Rnd 27: (Color 1 1 sc in each of next 3 sts, dec, Color 2 1 sc in each of next 4 sts) 6 times = 48 sts.

Rnd 28: (Color 1 1 sc in each of next 4 sts, dec, Color 2 1 sc in each of next 2 sts, dec) 6 times = 42 sts.

Rnd 29: (Color 1 1 sc in each of next 4 sts, dec, Color 2 1 sc in each of next 3 sts) 6 times = 42 sts.

Rnd 30: (Color 1 1 sc in each of next 2 sts, dec, Color 2 1 sc in each of next 3 sts) 6 times = 36 sts.

Rnd 31: (Color 1 1 sc in each of next 3 sts, dec, Color 2 1 sc in each of next 3 sts) 6 times = 36 sts.

Rnd 32: (Color 1 1 sc in each of next 3 sts, Color 2 1 sc in next st, dec) 6 times = 30 sts.

Rnd 33: (Color 1 1 sc in each of next 3 sts, dec, Color 2 1 sc in each of next 2 sts) 6 times = 30 sts.

Add fiberfill to ornament, filling it well so it assumes its proper shape, and so it doesn't lose its silhouette when you press on it. Weigh the fiberfill so you'll have the "just right" amount in each ornament.

Tip: It will be easier to embroider the stripes over the first 30 rounds at this point. Leave all the ends hanging so you can use them to embroider the remaining lengths of the stripes when you get to the last rnd. You can find suggestions for the stripes on page 40.

Rnd 34: (Color 1 1 sc in next st, dec, Color 2 1 sc in each of next 2 sts) 6 times = 24 sts.

Rnd 35: (Color 1 1 sc in each of next 2 sts, Color 2 1 sc in each of next 2 sts) 6 times = 24 sts.

Rnd 36: (Color 1 1 sc in each of next 2 sts, Color 2 dec) 6 times = 18 sts.

Rnd 37: (Color 1 1 sc in each of next 2 sts, Color 2 1 sc in next st) 6 times = 18 sts.

Rnd 38: (Color 1 dec, Color 2 1 sc in next st) 6 times = 12 sts.

Rnd 39: (Color 1 1 sc in next st, Color 2 1 sc in next st) 6 times = 12 sts.

The next 4 rnds are worked only with Color 1.

Rnd 40: (Dec, 1 sc in each of next 2 sts) 3 times = 9 sts.

Rnds 41–43: 1 sc in each st around = 9 sts.

Note: Work the last st on Rnd 43 as a sl st to level the transition between the beginning and end of the rnd.

Cut yarn and weave in ends on WS.

Fill the top of the ornament.

GOLD TOP

The gold top for the ornament is worked in rounds. Each rnd is joined with a sl st and begins with ch 1 to raise the height of the rnd. The first st of the rnd is worked into the same st as the sl st. Do not include the sl sts in stitch counts.

Work the top with Shiny Glimmergarn, color Gold.
Rnd 1: Work 6 sc around a magic ring. End with 1 sl st to join rnd = 6 sts.

Rnd 2: Ch 1, (inc) 6 times. End with 1 sl st to join rnd = 12 sts.

Work sts of next rnd through back loops to make a ridge so the edge of the top bends down sharply.

Rnd 3: Ch 1, 1 sc in BL of each st around. End with 1 sl st to join rnd = 12 sts.

Rnds 4–7: Ch 1, 1 sc in each st around. End with 1 sl st to join rnd = 12 sts.

Cut yarn, leaving an end long enough to sew top to ornament.

GOLD CORD

Make the cord with Shiny Glimmergarn, color Gold.
Make a firmly worked chain about 7" (18 cm) long. After you finish the chain, fold it at the center and make a knot at each end. The cord is then pulled through the crocheted top so the knot is placed in the top.

FINISHING

Place the gold top with the cord on top of the striped ornament. The base of the gold top should align with the top of Rnd 39—it is the last round crocheted with 2 colors. It helps to pin the pieces together.

Thread a needle with the same color yarn as for the top of the ornament. We recommend using a thin and sharp tip curved needle for sewing the pieces together.

Sew the top onto the ornament.

Weave in all ends on WS and cut yarn.

Once you've sewn the ornament together, you can squeeze and roll it into shape to look like the ornaments shown here.

EMBROIDERED STRIPES

You can make your ornaments even more decorative by embroidering Gold stripes down the lines where the colors change. Each stripe ends at the top of the Christmas ornament where the color changes end.

Weave in all ends on WS and cut yarn.

BOWS

Hanging bows on the Christmas tree is an old tradition that has been revived in many Christmas homes today. Bows can also decorate many of our other Christmas favorites, such as the Christmas tree, advent wreaths, pine branches, ornaments, and even vanilla wreath cookies. A large crocheted bow on a wreath is welcoming on the front door, and gifts can be personalized with homemade bows.

In this pattern, you will find instructions for three sizes of bow. They can be crocheted in many types of yarn and in every color, all depending on what type of Christmas home they'll decorate.

Skill Level

Bows are a project you can work on autopilot for most of the time. As soon as the pattern is memorized by your hands, you can mass-produce bows. Very little finishing is required and it is a project most can manage well.

How to Achieve Good Results

Bows are pretty, even when crocheted a little too loosely or tightly in respect to the given gauge. The tails fold most smoothly and are easiest to shape if all the pieces are wet-blocked before assembly.

Technique Videos for Bows

These are the techniques: Chain stitch, elongated single-crochet stitch, crocheting back and forth in rows, attaching yarn with a slip stitch, increasing, decreasing, crocheting in back loop, crocheting in front loop, crocheting in the loop on the back of a chain stitch, assembling the bow.

MATERIALS

Yarn

Small bow:
Organic Wool 1 (10 g)

Large bow:
Organic Wool 1 (38 g)

Extra-large bow:
One strand Organic Wool 1 (55g)
and
One strand Deluxe Silk Mohair (14 g)

TOOLS

Recommended crochet hook: U.S. size E-4 (3.5 mm) for small and large bows in Organic Wool 1 or U.S. G-6 (4 mm) for extra-large bow

Notions: Blunt tapestry needle for finishing, scissors

FINISHED MEASUREMENTS

Small bow: approx. 3¼" (8 cm) wide and 4" (10 cm) long with tails

Large bow: approx. 6" (15 cm) wide and 8" (20 cm) long with tails

Extra-large bow: 6¾" (17 cm) wide and 11½" (29 cm) long with tails

---

Gauge

26 sts × 40 rows crocheted in rows of elongated single crochet with Organic Wool 1 and hook U.S. size E-4 (3.5 mm) = 4" × 4" / 10 × 10 cm.

20 sts × 32 rows crocheted in rows of elongated single crochet with 1 strand each of Organic Wool 1 + Deluxe Silk Mohair and hook U.S. size G-6 (4 mm) = 4" × 4" / 10 × 10 cm.

Adjust hook size to obtain correct gauge if necessary.

Gauge is not important for good results with this project. Don't forget, though, that you will need more yarn if you crochet more loosely than at the gauge given above.

CONSTRUCTION

Each bow is crocheted in three pieces: the bow loop, the tails that hang from the loop, and a band to hold the pieces together.

Each piece is crocheted back and forth in rows of single crochet. The instructions indicate when every other single crochet should be worked as an elongated single crochet. An elongated single -crochet stitch (esc) is worked as for a normal single crochet, but, instead of inserting the hook under the top loop(s) of the stitch in the previous row, it is inserted into the base of that single crochet.

The pattern becomes obvious once the elongated single-crochet stitches have been worked over 2 rows.

To finish, make a row of single crochet all around the edges of the bow loop and tails. This creates a sharp and pretty look.

The first row is worked into the back of the chain stitches. The chain stitches should be a bit loose so you can easily insert the hook through them. If necessary, use a hook a quarter or half size larger for the foundation chain.

Turn each row with ch 1 as a turning chain.

Crochet Tips

The bow loop can be adjusted in length. If you want a plumper bow, you can make it shorter.

The small bow can be crocheted 4¾"–5½" (12–14 cm) long instead of 6¼" (16 cm). The large bow can be 8¾"–9½" (22–24 cm) long instead of 11¾" (30 cm). Th extra-large bow can be 10¼"–11" (26–28 cm) long instead of 14¼" (36 cm).

If you want shorter tails, repeat the pattern fewer times, before beginning the decreases.

SMALL BOW

Use hook U.S. size E-4 (3.5 mm) for Organic Wool 1 (or hook necessary for correct gauge).

Ch 10—the last ch is the turning ch.

Row 1: Beginning in 2nd ch from hook, work 1 sc in back of each ch = 9 sts.

Row 2: 1 sc in each st across = 9 sts.

Row 3: 1 esc in first st, (1 sc in next st, 1 esc in next st) 4 times = 9 sts.

Row 4: 1 sc in first st, (1 esc in next st, 1 sc in next st) 4 times = 9 sts.

Repeat Rows 3–4 until bow measures 6¼" (16 cm) total. End bow by working 1 row of sc. Cut yarn and weave in ends on WS.
Continue to section "Single-Crochet Edging for Bows" on next page.

LARGE AND EXTRA-LARGE BOWS

Use hook U.S. size E-4 (3.5 mm) for Organic Wool 1 (or hook necessary for correct gauge).

Ch 20—the last ch is the turning ch.

Row 1: Beginning in 2nd ch from hook, work 1 sc in back of each ch = 19 sts.

Row 2: 1 sc in each st across = 19 sts.

Row 3: 1 esc in first st, (1 sc in next st, 1 esc in next st) 9 times = 19 sts.

Row 4: 1 sc in first st, (1 esc in next st, 1 sc in next st) 9 times = 19 sts.

Repeat Rows 3–4 until large bow measures 11¾" (30 cm) total or extra-large bow measures 14¼" (36 cm). End bow by working 1 row of sc.

Cut yarn and weave in ends on WS.

Continue to section "Single-Crochet Edging for Bows" at right.

SINGLE-CROCHET EDGING FOR BOWS

For a nice finish on the bow, work a single-crochet edging along the long sides of the bow.

Make sure you don't crochet too tightly along the edges; otherwise, the bow will draw in. You might need to go up a quarter or half size up for your hook to make looser stitches.

Work the edging as follows:
Attach yarn with 1 sl st at one of the corners, where a short and long side meet.

Ch 1 in same st as sl st.
Work 1 sc for every 2 rows (1 sc for each hole in the row)—each st should be as wide as the row is high.
Cut yarn at end of long side and weave in end on WS.

Work a single-crochet edging on the other long side of the bow the same way.
Make sure you edge the long sides with the same side (RS) facing so the single-crochet edging will look the same on both edges.

TAILS

The tails are worked back and forth in rows from the center of the tail and out. The first 3–5 rows are worked in normal single crochet with increases on each side. Then the pattern begins. The tip of the tail is shaped with decreases on the last part of the piece.

Row 1 is worked in the loops on the back of the foundation chain. The chain should be a bit loose to keep it from drawing in.
If necessary, use a quarter or half size larger hook to make looser stitches.

Turn each row with ch 1 (turning chain).

The other end of the tail is worked directly from the foundation chain and continued as for the first part of the tail.

TAILS FOR THE SMALL BOW

Ch 4—the last ch is the turning ch.

Row 1: Beginning in 2nd ch from hook, work 1 sc in back of each ch = 3 sts.

Row 2: 1 sc in each st across = 3 sts.

Row 3: Inc, 1 sc in next st, inc = 5 sts.

Row 4: 1 sc in each st across = 5 sts.

Row 5: 1 esc in first st, (1 sc in next st, 1 esc in next st) 2 times = 5 sts.

Row 6: 1 sc in first st, (1 esc in next st, 1 sc in next st) 2 times = 5 sts.

Repeat Rows 5–6 until you've worked a total of 16 pattern rows (= 20 rows total).

On the next row, begin decreasing to shape tip. Decrease by skipping 1 st (sk-dec). When you decrease only on one side of the tail, that side will be diagonal. Turn each row with ch 1.

Row 21: Skip first st, (1 sc in next st, 1 esc in next st) 2 times = 4 sts.

Row 22: 1 sc in next sts, 1 esc in next st, sk-dec = 3 sts.

Row 23: Sk-dec, 1 esc in next st = 2 sts.

Row 24: Sk-dec = 1 st.

Row 25: 1 esc = 1 st.

Cut yarn but do not weave in ends.

Opposite Side of Tail—Small Bow

You've now finished the first half of the tail.
Turn work so the foundation chain is at the top and the tail points downward. At the same time, the end from the foundation chain should point to the right and the tip of the tail also points to the right. This way, the diagonal sides of the tails will be mirror-image.

Row 1: Attach yarn with 1 sl st to first st of foundation chain. Work 1 sc into same st as sl st and then work 1 sc in each of the last 2 sts on foundation ch = 3 sts.

Row 2: Inc, 1 sc in next st, inc = 5 sts.

Row 3: 1 sc in each st across = 5 sts.

Row 4: 1 esc in first st, (1 sc in next st, 1 esc in next st) 2 times = 5 sts.

Row 5: 1 sc in first st, (1 esc in next st, 1 sc in next st) 2 times = 5 sts.

Repeat Rows 4–5 until you've worked a total of 16 pattern rows (= 19 rows total).

On the next row, begin decreasing to shape tip. Decrease by skipping 1 st and working 1 sc in following st (sk-dec). When you decrease only on one side of the tail, that side will be diagonal. Turn each row with ch 1.

Row 20: Skip first st, (1 sc in next st, 1 esc in next st) 2 times = 4 sts.

Row 21: 1 sc in next sts, 1 esc in next st, sk dec = 3sts.

Row 22: Sk-dec, 1 esc in next st = 2 sts.

Row 23: Sk-dec = 1 st.

Row 24: 1 esc = 1 st.

Cut yarn and weave in end.

Continue to section "Single-Crochet Edging for Tails" on page 52.

TAILS FOR THE LARGE AND EXTRA-LARGE BOWS

Ch 8—the last ch is the turning ch.

Row 1: Beginning in 2nd ch from hook, work 1 sc in back of each ch = 7 sts.

Row 2: 1 sc in each st across = 7 sts.

Row 3: Inc, 1 sc in next of next 5 sts, inc = 9 sts.

Row 4: Inc, 1 sc in each of next 7 sts, inc = 11 sts.

Row 5: 1 sc in each st across = 11 sts.

Row 6: 1 esc in first st, (1 sc in next st, 1 esc in next st) 5 times = 11 sts.

Row 7: 1 sc in first st, (1 esc in next st, 1 sc in next st) 5 times = 11 sts.

Repeat Rows 6–7 until you've worked a total of 48 pattern rows (= 53 rows total).

On the next row, begin decreasing to shape tip. Decrease by skipping 1 st, 1 sc in next st (sk-dec). When you decrease only on one side of the tail, that side will be diagonal.
Turn each row with ch 1.

Row 54: Skip first st, (1 sc in next st, 1 esc in next st) 5 times = 10 sts.

Row 55: (1 sc in next sts, 1 esc in next st) 4 times, sk-dec = 9 sts.

Row 56: Sk-dec, (1 esc in next st, 1 sc in next st) 3times, 1 esc in next st = 8 sts.

Row 57: (1 sc in next st, 1 esc in next st) 3 times, sk-dec = 7 sts.

Row 58: Sk-dec, (1 esc in next st, 1 sc in next st) 2times, 1 esc in next st = 6 sts.

Row 59: (1 sc in next st, 1 esc in next st) 2 times, sk-dec = 5 sts.

Row 60: Sk-dec, 1 esc in next st, 1 sc in next st, 1 esc in next st = 4 sts.

Row 61: 1 sc in next st, 1 esc in next st, sk-dec = 3 sts.

Row 62: Sk-dec, 1 esc in next st = 2 sts.

Row 63: Sk-dec = 1 st.

Cut yarn but do not weave in end.

Opposite Side of Tail—Large and Extra-Large Bows

You've now finished the first half of the tail. Turn work so the foundation chain is at the top and the tail points downward. At the same time, the end from the foundation chain should point to the right and the tip of the tail also points to the right. This way, the diagonal sides of the tails will be mirror-image.

Row 1: Attach yarn with 1 sl st to first st of foundation chain. Work 1 sc into same st as sl st and then work 1 sc in each st on foundation ch = 7 sts.

Row 2: Inc, 1 sc in each of next 5 sts, inc = 9 sts.

Row 3: Inc, 1 sc in each of next 7 sts, inc = 11 sts.

Row 4: 1 sc in each st across = 11 sts.

Row 5: 1 esc in first st, (1 sc in next st, 1 esc in next st) 5 times = 11 sts.

Row 6: 1 sc in first st, (1 esc in next st, 1 sc in next st) 5 times = 11 sts.

Repeat Rows 5–6 until you've worked a total of 48 pattern rows (= 52 rows total).

On the next row, begin decreasing to shape tip. Decrease by skipping 1 st and working 1 sc in following st (sk-dec). When you decrease only on one side of the tail, that side will be diagonal. Turn each row with ch 1.

Row 53: Skip first st, (1 sc in next st, 1 esc in next st) 5 times = 10 sts.

Row 54: (1 sc in next sts, 1 esc in next st) 4 times, sk0 dec = 9 sts.

Row 55: Sk dec, (1 esc in next st, 1 sc in next st) 3 times, 1 esc in next st = 8 sts.

Row 56: (1 sc in next st, 1 esc in next st) 3 times, sk-dec = 7 sts.

Row 57: Sk-dec, (1 esc in next st, 1 sc in next st) 2 times, 1 esc in next st = 6 sts.

Row 58: (1 sc in next st, 1 esc in next st) 2 times, sk-dec = 5 sts.

Row 59: Skip 1 st, (1 sc in next st, 1 esc in next st) 2 times = 4 sts.

Row 60: 1 sc in next st, 1 esc in next st, sk-dec = 3 sts.

Row 61: Sk dec, 1 esc in next st = 2 sts.

Row 62: 1-sk dec = 1 st.

Row 63: 1 esc = 1 st.

Cut yarn and weave in end. Continue to section "Single-Crochet Edging for Tails" on next page.

SINGLE-CROCHET EDGING FOR TAILS

For a nice finish on the tails, work a single-crochet edging along the long sides of each tail.

Make sure you don't crochet too tightly along the edges; otherwise, the tail will draw in. If necessary, use a quarter or half size larger hook to make looser stitches.

The diagonal edge of each tail should point toward the center of the bow, but the diagonals will point up and outward while you work the single-crochet edging so the right side of the edging will face correctly.

If you want the diagonals to point away from the center of the bow, work the edging with the diagonals pointing up and inward so the right side of the edging will face correctly,

Work the edging as follows:
Attach yarn with 1 sl st at the foundation chain at the center of the piece, where the tails meet.

Ch 1 in same st as sl st.
Work 1 sc for every 2 rows (1 sc for each hole in the row)—each st should be as wide as the row is high.

At the rounding, where the pattern begins, work 2 sc in the same place to nicely round the space.

Make sure that the tips and corners of the tails stay pointed and sharp. You can do this by either working 3 sc or (1 sc, ch 1, 1 sc) at each place where you need a sharp corner.
Once you've crocheted the edging all the way around the tail, cut yarn and weave in ends on WS.

CENTER BAND

Make a small band to place around and hold the bow and tails together. The band is a strip worked back and forth in single crochet.

The band should be just long enough to wrap around the bow and tails. If it is a bit too loose, you can overlap the ends more. If it is too short, begin with more stitches than specified for working a longer band.
The band for a small bow should be about 3" (7.5 cm) long while the band for the larger bows should be approx. 4¼" and 4¾" (11 and 12 cm).

Row 1 is worked into the back of the foundation chain. This makes a smooth and uniform edge on the top and bottom of the band.
Make sure that you crochet loosely enough so the foundation chain doesn't draw in.
If necessary, use a quarter or half size larger hook to make looser stitches for the foundation chain.

Turn each row with ch 1.

BAND FOR SMALL BOW

Ch 13—the last st is the turning ch.

Row 1: Beginning in 2nd ch from hook, work 1 sc in each loop on back of chain row = 12 sts.

Row 2: Work 1 sc in each st across = 12 sts.

Cut yarn, leaving one end long enough to seam band.

Weave in yarn end from foundation chain.

BAND FOR LARGE AND EXTRA-LARGE BOWS

Ch 21—the last st is the turning ch.

Row 1: Beginning in 2nd ch from hook, work 1 sc in each loop on back of foundation chain = 20 sts.

Rows 2–4: Work 1 sc in each st across = 20 sts.

Cut yarn, leaving one end long enough to seam band.

Weave in yarn end from foundation chain.

WASHING AND BLOCKING

You can obtain a pretty and even result for your finished project if you block the individual pieces before you seam them together.
If you don't block them before assembly, the tails will usually roll in and it will be difficult to get them to hang down straight.

ASSEMBLY

After all the pieces have been crocheted and blocked, you can assemble them into a bow.

STEP 1

Thread a needle with the same color yarn as for the bow. Fold the short sides of the bow in toward each other. If necessary, hold the piece together with a couple of pins.
Sew the ends together from the top down to the base to form a ring. Do not cut yarn.

Place the seam at center back of the bow.

Wrap the yarn end from the seaming around the center of the bow a couple of times to shape the middle. Don't wrap too firmly and, at the same time, make sure that the edges of the long sides point back toward the back of the bow. This last advice is especially important for the larger bows.

Knot the yarn a couple of times where it is wrapped around the bow and weave in ends.

STEP 2

Fold the tail piece at the center so that the single-crochet edging's right side points forward and the tips' diagonal sides either point in toward the middle of the bow or away from the bow's middle. Place the tail up on the base of the bow and fold the band around both the bow and tails.
It can be helpful if you hold the pieces together with pins. Avoid tightening the band too firmly around the bow and tails. It should look plump and airy without gaping or being loose.

The tails for the large bow can even be folded at the center on the long sides before the band is sewn on. This makes the tails look plumper up at the bow.

STEP 3

Seam the band ends. If the band is too long, you can overlap the ends when you sew them.

GINGERBREAD HOUSE

It is the height of hygge coziness to bake a gingerbread house and decorate it with your favorite sweet embellishments. A crocheted one that can be decorated and used as a lovely little light box creates a cozy Christmas feeling in the elf landscape, on the Christmas table, and on a windowsill.

Skill Level

So that the various pieces of the gingerbread house will fit together well, it is important to be able to crochet evenly and uniformly, but: there are no challenging crochet techniques for making the gingerbread house. You'll crochet simply with the most common crochet techniques: decreases and increases, and basic stitches, which the vast majority of crocheters are familiar with. In general, there is a good deal of assembly, which will require some patience because there are many parts that need to be sewn together with needle and thread.

Pssst . . . You can also cheat a bit with the assembly by gluing some of the pieces, if assembly is not your thing.

How to Achieve Good Results

For this project, good results will come from carefully crocheting tightly and evenly and taking your time when assembling all the various pieces. The house will look especially sharp if chipboard is glued on to reinforce all the surfaces of the house.

Technique Videos for the Gingerbread House

These are the techniques: Chain stitch, single crochet, half-double crochet, double crochet, elongated single-crochet, attaching yarn with a slip stitch, magic ring, crocheting back and forth in rows, crocheting around in a spiral, crocheting in the loop on the back of a chain stitch, increasing, decreasing, icicles, spruce branches, embroidered stripes, French knots, assembly of the gingerbread house.

MATERIALS

Yarn and Notions

Organic Cotton

Gingerbread house walls and roof: 60 g color 30, Brown

Snow, icicles, and candy canes: 20 g color 01 Natural White

Door, candy canes, and red mini Christmas balls on the spruce branches: 5 g color 35, Red

Spruce branches and door wreath: 10 g color 36, Army Green

Pipe cleaners for stiffening the candy canes.

TOOLS

Recommended crochet hook: U.S. steel size 4 (2 mm)

Notions: Chipboard (single ply cardboard) for stiffening the walls (for example, the back board of a paper tablet)

PVA craft glue (for example, school glue)

Scissors

FINISHED MEASUREMENTS

The gingerbread house is approx. 4" (10 cm) wide, 5⅛"–5½" (13–14 cm) long, and 5¼" (13.5 cm) high when it has been assembled.

Gauge

38 sts × 40 rows crocheted back and forth in single crochet and hook U.S. steel size 4 (2 mm) = 4" × 4" / 10 × 10 cm.

Adjust hook size to obtain correct gauge if necessary.

The gingerbread house can be crocheted a little more loosely than at the given gauge. In that case, it is important to reinforce the house following the suggestions given in the pattern.

To achieve a firm gauge with Organic Cotton, use a small size hook, for example U.S. steel 4 (2 mm). However, a smaller size than that is not recommended as the hook might be too small for catching the yarn.

Chart

GINGERBREAD HOUSE

CHART 1—WALL

Row 1 and following odd-numbered rows = WS of wall.

Row 2 and following even-numbered rows = RS of wall.

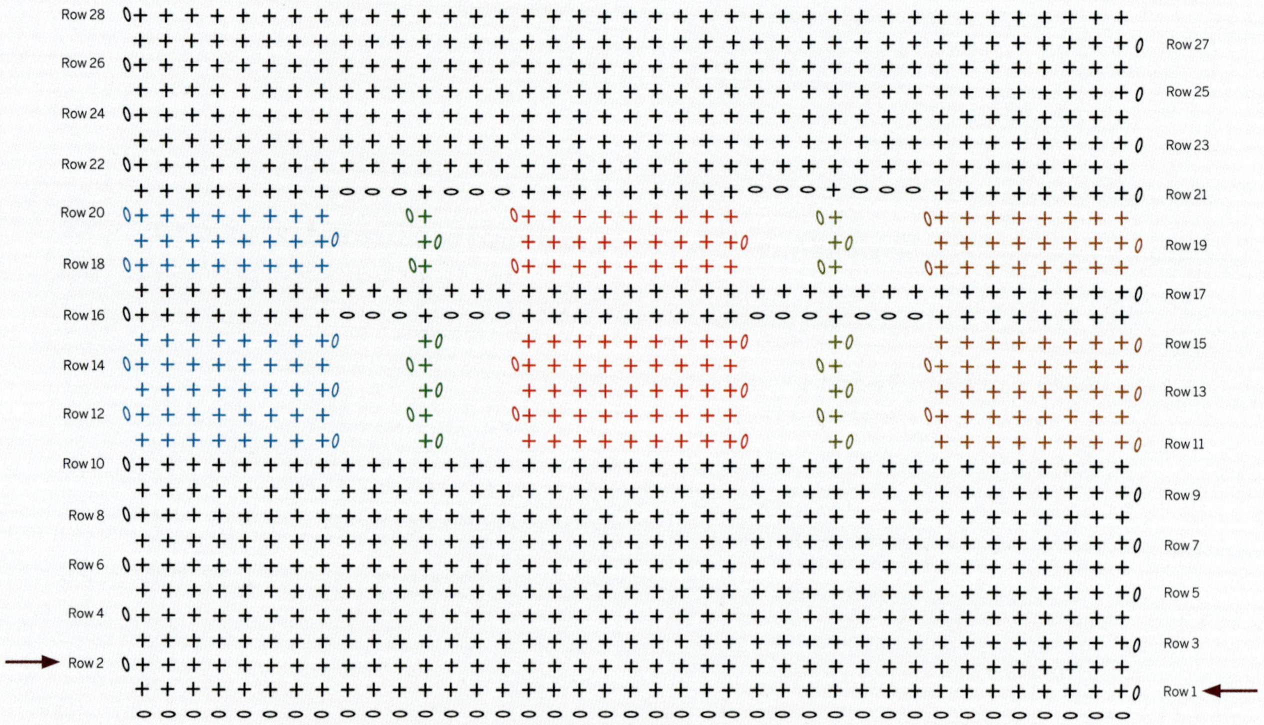

■ = Section 1: Wall on right side of right window as seen from WS.

■ = Section 2: Vertical window bars of right window as seen from WS.

■ = Section 3: Wall between right and left windows as seen from WS.

■ = Section 4: Vertical window bars of left window as seen from WS.

■ = Section 5: Wall on left side of left window as seen from WS.

← = Chart is read from right to left and crocheted on WS of work.

→ = Chart is read from left to right and crocheted on RS of work.

CONSTRUCTION

The gingerbread house is constructed in several different steps and pieces.

All of the pieces are crocheted separately and assembled afterward.

Step 1: Walls, end gables
Step 2: Windows
Step 3: Door
Step 4: Spruce branches
Step 5: Roof surface
Step 6: Candy canes
Step 7: Snowdrifts
Step 8: Icicles
Step 9: Assembly

Before you begin crocheting the individual pieces, it is important that you first read through each section. These sections include information about what you should be aware of for making each of the separate pieces.

Crochet Tips

Even though there are many small pieces to be assembled, they will be joined only with simple back stitch. Many of the pieces can be glued instead of being sewn, but, the nicest results will come from following the assembly methods explained in the pattern.

WALLS WITH WINDOWS

The walls are crocheted back and forth in single crochet from the bottom up. Each row is turned with ch 1 as the turning stitch.

To crochet the windows, the piece is divided into five sections on Row 11 and again on Row 18. On Rows 16 and 21, all the sections are joined with chain stitch. Then, you can once again crochet over all the stitches on the following rows.

Row 1 is worked into the back loops on the foundation chain. The chain should be worked a bit loosely but will be pulled in once it is crocheted into. We recommend using a hook a quarter or half size larger for the foundation chain.

Important:
In principle, either side can be considered as the right side, but, it is important to note that the written text and charts have, as the starting point, that Row 1 is the wrong side and Row 2 is therefore the right side, the side that will face out when the gingerbread house is assembled.

The chart and text follow a row sequence, with the piece beginning on Row 1, the wrong side, when the house is assembled. This is particularly important to note when the piece is sectioned for the first time on Row 11 for the windows and wall.

When the piece is divided for the windows on row 18, you should be crocheting on the right side. The 5th section is the last section of the piece on the wrong side; the 5th section will be the first on the right side.

With Brown, ch 40—the last ch is the turning chain.

Row 1: Beginning in 2nd ch from hook, work 1 sc in each loop on back of foundation chain = 39 sts.

Rows 2–10: Work back and forth with 1 sc in each st across = 39 sts.

On the next row, divide the piece into 5 sections to make the lower window frames. As seen from the WS, crochet in the following sequence:

Section 1: Wall on right side of right window.
Section 2: Vertical window bar of right window.
Section 3: Wall between right and left windows.
Section 4: Vertical window bar of left window.
Section 5: Wall on left side of left window.

Continue with ch 1 as turning ch on each row.

Crochet Tips

You can crochet over the yarn end from the foundation chain, when working a new section of the piece.

That way, the end is woven in as you work. Make sure that all the stitches on this row are worked extra firmly, so the row won't be higher when the end is encased in the crochet stitches. At the window bars, the ends can be woven in later so they won't be encased under just one single-crochet stitch but will simply be held in place.

SECTION 1: WALL ON THE RIGHT SIDE OF THE RIGHT WINDOW

Row 11: Work 1 sc in each of the first 8 sts = 8 sts.

Turn and work back over the 8 sts:
Rows 12–15: 1 sc in each of the first 8 sts = 8 sts.

Cut yarn and weave in end on WS or down through end sts on left side of wall.

SECTION 2: VERTICAL WINDOW BAR OF RIGHT WINDOW

When beginning a new section in the middle of the piece, attach the yarn with 1 sl st into the st indicated. The 1st st of the row is worked into same st as sl st.

Row 11: Attach yarn with 1 sl st into 4th st to left of Section 1. There are 12 sts on wall, Row 10. Work 1 sc in same st as sl st = 1 st.

Turn and work back:
Rows 12–15: 1 sc = 1 st.

Cut yarn and weave in end on WS or down through sts on left side of frame.
Also weave in the end from the beginning end through the sts on right side of the frame and up.

SECTION 3: WALL BETWEEN RIGHT AND LEFT WINDOWS

Row 11: Attach yarn with 1 sl st into 4th st to left of window frame st. There are 16 sts on wall, Row 10. Work 1 sc in same st as sl st = 1 st, 1 sc in each of next 8 sts = 9 sts.

Rows 12–15: 1 sc in each st across section = 9 sts.

Cut yarn and weave in end on WS or down through sts on left side of wall.
Also weave in the end from the beginning end through the sts on right side of the wall and up, if you didn't cover end when crocheting Row 11.

SECTION 4: VERTICAL WINDOW BAR OF LEFT WINDOW

Row 11: Attach yarn with 1 sl st into 4th st to left of Section 3. There are 28 sts on wall, Row 10. Work 1 sc in same st as sl st = 1 st.

Rows 12–15: 1 sc = 1 st.

Cut yarn and weave in end on WS or down through sts on left side of frame.
Also weave in the end from the beginning end through the st on right side of the frame and up.

SECTION 5: THE WALL ON THE LEFT SIDE OF THE LEFT WINDOW

Row 11: Attach yarn with 1 sl st into 4th st to left of window frame st. There are 32 sts on wall, Row 10. Work 1 sc in same st as sl st = 1 st. Work 1 sc into each of next 7 sts = 8 sts.

Rows 12–15: 1 sc in each st = 8 sts.

Do not cut yarn, but continue to Row 16.

On the next row, the 5 sections are joined. You'll work ch sts from the walls in to the vertical frames and from the frames out to the walls.
This way, you will crochet once again over all the sts on Row 17 and the horizontal frames will be made for the windows.

Row 16: Turn and work back over all the sts as follows:
1 sc in each of the next 8 sts of wall (Section 5).
Ch 3.
1 sc in vertical bar of left window (Section 4).
Ch 3.
1 sc in each of the next 9 sts of wall (Section 3).
Ch 3.
1 sc in vertical bar of right window (Section 2).
Ch 3.
1 sc in each of the next 8 sts of wall (Section 1) = 39 sts total.

On next row, work over all the sts.
The windows stand out most if they are crocheted in the loop on back side of each chain st, but, it is also possible to crochet through or around the entire ch.

Row 17: Turn and work back over all the sts as follows:
1 sc in each of the next 8 sts of wall (Section 1).
1 sc in each of the 3 ch.
1 sc in vertical bar of right window (Section 2).
1 sc in each of the 3 ch.
1 sc in each of the next 9 sts of wall (Section 3).
1 sc in each of the 3 ch.
1 sc in vertical bar of left window (Section 4).
1 sc in each of the 3 ch.
1 sc in each of the next 8 sts of wall (Section 5) = 39 sts total.

On the next row, once again divide the piece into 5 sections to make the top frames of the windows. The divisions are made on RS of work, so, you will crochet across in the direction opposite that done previously for the larger frame pieces.

Section 1: Wall on left side of left window.
Section 2: Vertical window bar of left window.
Section 3: Wall between left and right windows.
Section 4: Vertical window bar of right window.
Section 5: Wall on right side of right window.

Continue with ch 1 as turning ch on each row.

SECTION 5: THE WALL ON THE LEFT SIDE OF THE LEFT WINDOW

Row 18: Work 1 sc into each of first 8 sts = 8 sts.

Rows 19–20: 1 sc in each st = 8 sts.

Cut yarn and weave in end on WS or down through sts on left side of wall.

SECTION 4: VERTICAL WINDOW BAR OF LEFT WINDOW

Row 18: Attach yarn with 1 sl st into 4th st to left of Section 5. There are 12 sts on wall, Row 17. Work 1 sc in same st as sl st = 1 st.

Rows 19–20: 1 sc = 1 st.

Cut yarn and weave in end on WS or down through sts on left side of frame.
Also weave in the end from the beginning end through the st on right side of the frame and up.

SECTION 3: WALL BETWEEN LEFT AND RIGHT WINDOWS

Row 18: Attach yarn with 1 sl st into 4th st to left of window bar st. There are 16 sts on wall, Row 17. Work 1 sc in same st as sl st, 1 sc in each of next 8 sts = 9 sts.

Rows 19–20: 1 sc in each st across section = 9 sts.

Cut yarn and weave in end on WS or down through sts on left side of wall.
Also weave in the end from the beginning end through the st on right side of the wall and up.

SECTION 2: VERTICAL WINDOW BAR OF RIGHT WINDOW

Row 18: Attach yarn with 1 sl st into 4th st to left of Section 3. There are 28 sts on wall, Row 17. Work 1 sc in same st as sl st = 1 st.

Rows 19–20: 1 sc = 1 st.

Cut yarn and weave in end on WS or down through sts on left side of wall.
Also weave in the end from the beginning end through the st on right side of wall and up, if you didn't crochet over it on Row 18.

SECTION 1: WALL ON THE RIGHT SIDE OF THE RIGHT WINDOW

Row 18: Attach yarn with 1 sl st into 4th st to left of window frame. There are 32 sts on wall, Row 17. Work 1 sc in same st as sl st. Work 1 sc in each of the next 7 sts = 8 sts.

Rows 19–20: 1 sc in each st across section = 8 sts.

Do not cut yarn, but continue to Row 21.

On the next row, the 5 sections are joined as you did for the large panes on Row 16.

Row 21: Turn and work back over all the sts as follows:
1 sc in each of the next 8 sts of wall (Section 1).
Ch 3.
1 sc in vertical bar of right window (Section 2).
Ch 3.
1 sc in each of the next 9 sts of wall (Section 2).
Ch 3.
1 sc in vertical bar of left window (Section 4).
Ch 3.
1 sc in each of the next 8 sts of wall (Section 5)
= 39 sts total.

On next row, work over all the sts.
The windows stand out most if they are crocheted in the loop on back side of each chain st, but, it is also possible to crochet through or around the entire ch loop.

Row 22: Turn and work back over all the sts as follows:
1 sc in each of the next 8 sts of wall (Section 5).
1 sc in each of the 3 ch.
1 sc in vertical bar of left window (Section 4).
1 sc in each of the 3 ch.
1 sc in each of the next 9 sts of wall (Section 3).
1 sc in each of the 3 ch.
1 sc in vertical bar of right window (Section 2).
1 sc in each of the 3 ch.
1 sc in each of the next 8 sts of wall (Section 1)
= 39 sts total.

Rows 23–28: 1 sc in each st across = 39 sts.

Cut yarn and weave in ends.

Crochet a total of two walls the same way and then continue to the section, "Single-Crochet Edging along Short Sides of Walls" below.

SINGLE-CROCHET EDGING ALONG SHORT SIDES OF WALLS

To stabilize the sides of the walls and make it easier to sew them together, work single-crochet edgings on the short sides of each wall.
Work edging with RS facing you. On the right side, crochet from the bottom up and, on the left side, from the top down.

The number of stitches to crochet depends on how the stitches are placed and how tightly they are worked. The edging should neither ruffle nor draw in. A starting point would be: work 1 sc for each row, at the same time, skipping 1 st every 4th–5th row.

If the edging ruffles, there are too many stitches. If the edging draws in, there are too few stitches. At the same time, it is important to have the same number of stitches on each side so you can match them up evenly when seaming.
Use stitch markers to indicate each stitch that was skipped so you can do the same thing on each side.

Work as follows:
Use the same color as for the walls.
Attach yarn with 1 sl st in the lower right corner on RS of wall. Work 1 sc in the same st as sl st.
Continue working sc all along the entire side.

Cut yarn and weave in ends on WS of wall.

END GABLE WITH WINDOW

The end gables are worked back and forth in single crochet in rows from the bottom and up, the same way as for the walls. You will make only one window, instead of two.

The piece is divided into three sections for the window and walls on Row 11 and again on Row 18. On Rows 16 and 21, all the sections are joined with chain stitches. You can then crochet across all the stitches on the following row as for the walls.

Even-numbered rows are on the RS when the gingerbread house is assembled. The text and charts are seen and explained from the wrong side.

Ch 26—the last st is a turning st.
Row 1: Beginning in 2nd ch from hook, work 1 sc in back loop of each ch = 25 sts.

Rows 2–10: 1 sc in each st across = 25 sts.
On the next row, divide the piece into 3 sections to make the lower panes of the window.

Section 1: Wall on right side of window.
Section 2: Vertical window bar of window.
Section 3: Wall on left side of window.
Turn each row with ch 1.

SECTION 1: WALL ON RIGHT SIDE OF WINDOW

Row 11: 1 sc in each of first 9 sts = 9 sts.

Rows 12–15: 1 sc in each st across = 9 sts.

Cut yarn and weave in end either on WS of wall or down through sts on left side of wall.

SECTION 2: VERTICAL WINDOW BAR OF WINDOW

Row 11: Attach yarn with 1 sl st into 4th st to left of Section 1. There are 13 sts on wall Row 10. Work 1 sc in same st as sl st = 1 st.

Rows 12–15: 1 sc = 1 st.

Cut yarn and weave in end either on WS of wall or down through sts on left side of window bar. Also, weave in beginning yarn end through sst of right side of frame and up.

SECTION 3: WALL ON LEFT SIDE OF WINDOW

Row 11: Attach yarn with 1 sl st into 4th st to left of window bar st. There are 17 sts on wall Row 10. Work 1 sc in same st as sl st, 1 sc in each of next 8 sts = 9 sts.

Turn and work back.
Rows 12–15: 1 sc in each st across = 9 sts.

Do not cut yarn. Continue to Row 16.

On the next row, the 3 sections are joined. You'll work chain stitches from the wall in to the vertical bar and out to the wall. This way, you will be again able to crochet over all the sts on Row 17 where the horizontal bar is made in the window.

Chart

GINGERBREAD HOUSE

CHART 2—END GABLE

Row 1 and following odd-numbered rows = WS of wall.
Row 2 and following even-numbered rows = RS of wall.

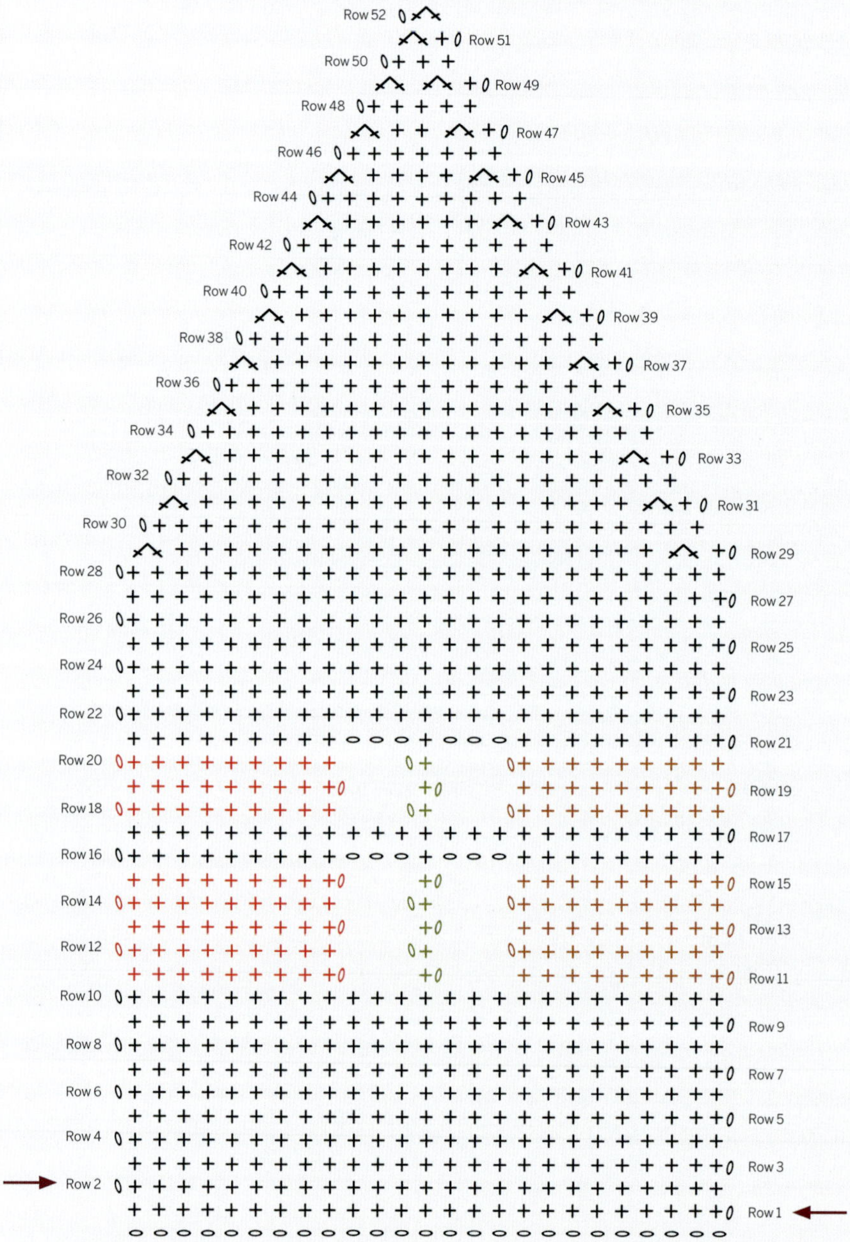

- ■ = Section 1: Wall on right side of window as seen from WS.
- ■ = Section 2: Vertical window bar of right window.
- ■ = Section 3: Wall on left side of window as seen from WS.

← = Chart is read from right to left and crocheted on WS of work.

→ = Chart is read from left to right and crocheted on RS of work.

Row 16: Turn and work back over all sts as follows:
1 sc in each of the next 9 sts of wall (Section 3).
Ch 3.
1 sc in vertical bar of window (Section 2).
Ch 3.
1 sc in each of the next 9 sts of wall (Section 1).
= 25 sts.

On the next row, work over all the sts.
The window will stand out most if it is crocheted in the loop on back side of each chain st, but, it is also possible to crochet through or around the entire ch loop.
Row 17: Turn and work over all the sts as follows:
1 sc in each of the next 9 sts of wall (Section 1).
1 sc in each of the 3 ch.
1 sc in vertical bar of window (Section 2).
1 sc in each of the 3 ch.
1 sc in each of the next 9 sts of wall (Section 3).
= 25 sts.

On the next row, once again divide the piece into 3 sections to make the top bar of the windows.
The divisions are made on RS of work, so, you will crochet across in the direction opposite that done previously for the larger frame pieces.

Section 3: Wall on left side of left window.
Section 2: Vertical window bar.
Section 1: Wall on right side of right window.

Turn each row with ch 1.

SECTION 3: WALL ON LEFT SIDE OF LEFT WINDOW

Row 18: 1 sc in each of the first 9 sts = 9 sts.

Rows 19–20: 1 sc in each st across = 9 sts.

Cut yarn. Weave in end either on WS of wall or down through sts on left side of wall.

SECTION 2: VERTICAL WINDOW BAR

Row 18: Attach yarn with 1 sl st in 4th st to left of section 3. There are 13 sts on wall Row 17.
1 sc in same st as sl st = 1 st.

Rows 19–20: 1 sc = 1 st.

Cut yarn. Weave in end either on WS of wall or down through sts on left side of frame.
Also weave in yarn end from beginning of frame st through sts on right side of bar and up.

SECTION 1: WALL ON RIGHT SIDE OF LEFT WINDOW

Row 18: Attach yarn with 1 sl st in 4th st to left of window bar st. There are 17 sts on wall Row 17.
1 sc in same st as sl st. 1 sc in eac of nexy 8 sts = 9 sts.

Rows 19–20: 1 sc in st across = 9 sts.

Do not cut yarn. Continue to Row 21.

On the next row, the 3 sections are joined as you did for the large frame piece on Row 16.

Row 21: Turn and work back over all the sts as follows:
1 sc in each of next 9 sts of wall (Section 1).
Ch 3.
1 sc in st of vertical window bar (Section 2).
Ch 3.
1 sc in each of next 9 sts of wall (Section 3).

= 25 sts.
On next row, crochet across all the sts.
The window will stand out most if it is crocheted in the loop on back side of each chain st, but, it is also possible to crochet through or around the entire
ch loop.

Row 22:
1 sc in each of next 9 sts of wall (Section 3).
1 sc in each ch 3 loop.
1 sc in st of vertical window bar (Section 2).
1 sc in each ch 3 loop.
1 sc in each of next 9 sts of wall (Section 1).
= 25 sts.

Rows 23–28: 1 sc in each st across = 25 sts.

On the next row, you'll begin decreasing to shape the tip of the end gable. Decrease on each side of the piece by skipping 1 st and then working 1 sc in next st.
Row 29: 1 sc, sk-dec, 1 sc in each st until 2 sts rem, sk-dec = 23 sts.

Row 30: 1 sc in each st across = 23 sts.

Work Rows 29–30 a total of 10 times, until 5 sts rem.

Row 49: 1 sc in next st, (sk-dec) 2 times = 3 sts.

Row 50: 1 sc in each st across = 3 sts.

Row 51: 1 sc in next st, sk-dec = 2 sts.

Row 52: Sk-dec = 1 st.
Cut yarn and weave in ends.
Continue to section "Single-Crochet Edging for End Gable" at right.

END GABLE WITHOUT A WINDOW

Ch 26 sts—the last st is a turning st.
Row 1: Beginning in 2nd ch from hook, work 1 sc in loop on back of each ch = 25 sts.

Rows 2–28: 1 sc in each st across = 25 sts.

Now shape tip of gable, decreasing as you did on Rows 29–52 of End Gable with a Window.

SINGLE-CROCHET EDGING FOR END GABLES

To stabilize the sides of the gables and make it easier to sew them together, work single-crochet edgings around the wall and roof.

Work edging with RS facing you. Begin on lower right side and crochet from the bottom up, around the roof, and down the left side.

The number of stitches to crochet depends on how the stitches are placed and how tightly they are worked. The edging should neither ruffle nor draw in. A starting point would be: work 1 sc for each row, at the same time, skipping 1 st every 4th–5th row.

If the edging ruffles, there are too many stitches. If the edging draws in, there are too few stitches. At the same time, it is important to have the same number of stitches on each side so you can match them up evenly when seaming.

Work as follows:
Use the same color yarn as for the end gables.
Attach yarn with 1 sl st in lower right corner on RS of gable.
Work 1 sc in same st as sl st.
Continue, working sc along the whole side.

At the corner, where the roof tip starts, work 2 sc in the hole between Rows 28 and 29 to round the corner.

The tip of the end gable should be as pointed as possible. You can do this by working 1 sc as far out into the point as possible. Then ch 1, followed by 1 sc in the post of the previous sc.
Continue along the left side of the roof and down along the left wall.
Do not work along the base of the gable.

When you've finished crocheting along the sides and roof, cut the yarn and weave in the ends on WS of gable.

BLOCKING

The walls and end gables will look nice and be uniform if they are blocked before the next pieces are crocheted and assembled.

WINDOWS

The windows consist of absolutely simple chain stitch rows, for both the window frames and window bars.

The bars do require a little care to crochet and sew. The more firmly you crochet, the easier it will be to make the assembly neat and uniform.

Once the window frames and bars ae assembled, you can iron or press them carefully.

Crochet Tips

The assembly will be much easier if the walls and windows are blocked beforehand.

VERTICAL WINDOW BARS

With Natural White, ch 10 sts—or the number of sts for a chain that is 1 ch longer than the vertical window bar.

Cut yarn and draw end through last chain st loop.

Sew on the bar securely as follows:
Thread a needle with the beginning yarn end.
Lay chain for vertical window bar so RS is facing, with the beginning foundation st is at the bottom and the last st at the top.

Insert needle into house wall in the ridge between Rows 10 and 11 directly below the vertical bar. Use back stitch to sew up and down in the center of the ch all the way up until 2–3 ch remain.

Weave in yarn end on WS of piece.

Thread a needle with yarn end from last ch. Insert needle in ridge directly over bar between Rows 22 and 23.

Now sew the last chain together with the bar as before. Weave in yarn end on WS.

HORIZONTAL WINDOW BARS

Use Natural White.
The horizontal bars are crocheted directly on the already-assembled vertical window bars.
Hold the piece so the horizontal bars lie vertical and the vertical bars are horizontal.

Insert the crochet hook into the ch that lies out in front of the small bar.
Attach yarn with 1 sl st and ch 3 or the number of ch sts needed for a chain row to cover the small bar.

Cut yarn and draw end though last ch loop.

Thread a needle with yarn end from last ch. Insert needle in stitch hole on wall directly at the side of the window bar.

Sew the chain to the bar as before for the vertical bars. Weave in ends on WS.

Weave in end from beginning chain st.

Turn work and continue the same way on the other little bar.

WINDOW FRAME

With Natural White, ch 38 or the number of sts necessary for a chain all around the window. The yarn end from the beginning ch should be long enough to sew the entire chain around the window.

Cut yarn and draw end though last ch loop.

Sew window frame securely around the window as for the bars. Make sure that the corners are sharp.

Crochet Tips

If you have made too many or too few chain stitches, you can undo any extra stitches or crochet a few more rather than unravelling the entire chain.

DOOR

The door is crocheted back and forth in rows of single crochet. The rounded top of the door is created with increases and decreases.
The door is finished with a single-crochet edging all around it to create a sharp and uniform finish.

Row 1 is worked in the loops on the back of the foundation chain. The chain should be worked a bit loosely because it will draw in when it is crocheted into. If necessary, use a hook a quarter or half size larger for the foundation chain.
The even-numbered rows are the RS of the door. This is important for when the single-crochet edging is worked and the door sewn onto the end gable.

Every row turns with ch 1.

With Red, ch 16—the last st is a turning ch.

Row 1: Beginning in 2nd ch from hook, work 1 sc in each loop on back of foundation chain = 15 sts.

Row 2: Inc, 1 sc in each st across = 16 sts.

Row 3: 1 sc in each of next 15 sts, inc = 17 sts.

Row 4: Inc, 1 sc in each st across = 18 sts.

Rows 5–7: 1 sc in each st across = 18 sts.

Row 8: Sk-dec, 1 sc in each st across = 17 sts.

Row 9: 1 sc in each of next 15 sts, sk-dec = 16 sts.

Row 10: Sk-dec, 1 sc in each st across = 15 sts.

Cut yarn and weave in ends on WS.

SINGLE-CROCHET EDGING

Finish the door by crocheting a single-crochet edging all around the doorframe.

Use the same color as for the door.
Attach yarn with 1 sl st at the center of the base, on RS. Work 1 sc in same st as sl st.

Continue, working sc to corner.
At the corner, ch 1 to round corner.
On the long side, work 1 sc in each st to rounding.
At door rounding, at some spots, work 2 sc into same spot to round the shaping.
Where exactly the sc should be placed depends on the width of the stitch. A starting point would be to work 2 sc in the same place 3–4 times across the door rounding.
On the opposite long side, work 1 sc in each st to the corner.

Ch 1 to round corner and then continue in sc along base to beginning of edging.

Once you've worked sc along the sides, top, and base, cut yarn and weave in ends on WS of door.

BLOCKING DOOR

Thread a needle with same color as door.
Knot 1 end.
Place the door centered on the end gable without a window and sew it on firmly with back stitch up and down along the top of the edging sts.
Sew all the way around. Cut yarn and weave in ends on WS of end gable.

SPRUCE BRANCHES

The spruce branches are placed around the windows and door for a cozy and Christmassy look. The branches are a simplified version of a crochet picot edging. They are crocheted directly into the foundation chain to make them as thin as possible and then sewn on to the windows and door.

The wreath on the door is a little spruce branch shaped into a circle. The wreath is embellished with small, red mini Christmas balls embroidered with French knots.

All the slip stitches are worked into the loops on the back of the foundation chain. The chain stitches should be somewhat loose because the chain will draw in once it is crocheted into. If necessary, use a crochet hook a quarter or half size larger for the foundation chain.

The spruce branch begins in the 2nd loop of the foundation chain.

SPRUCE BRANCHES FOR THE WINDOWS

With Army Green, ch 47 sts. Work 22 picots across (see next page).
Leave an end on the foundation chain long enough to use for sewing the branches to the wall.

Make a total of five spruce branches.

SPRUCE BRANCHES FOR THE DOOR

With Army Green, ch 57 sts. Work 27 picots across (see next page).
Leave an end on the foundation chain long enough to use for sewing the branches to the end gable.

SPRUCE BRANCHES FOR THE WREATH

With Army Green, ch 17 sts. Work 7 picots across (see next page).
Leave an end on the foundation chain long enough to use for sewing the branches into a ring and then to the door.

CHART 3—SPRUCE BRANCH

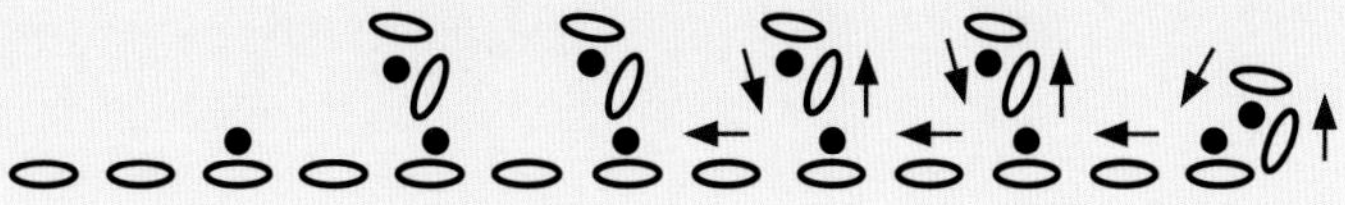

0 = Chain st
● = Slip st
→ = Direction of crochet

CROCHETED PICOTS

First picot on row:
1 sl st into 2nd ch from hook.
1 sl st into next ch.
Skip 1 ch.
1 sl st into next ch.

Remaining picots
Ch 2, 1 sl st into 2nd ch from hook.
Skip 1 ch.
1 sl st into next ch.

Repeat picots across row.

ASSEMBLY OF SPRUCE BRANCHES

Place the branches around the window/door so the picot tips point away from the window/door and the foundation chain firmly abuts the window/door edging.

If necessary, pin the branches on to keep them in place as you attach them.

Thread a needle with the end from the foundation chain and stitch across each picot—the stitch is placed on the base (at the chain st) and up to the tip. Stitch down each picot around the branch.

When the last picot has been stitched in place, pull it over to the first picot to close up the space between the beginning and end.

For the wreath, it will be easiest to sew along the inner circle of the ring so the picot tips will stick out slightly.

Weave in all the ends on WS of wall. Make a tiny bow to sew or glue onto the wreath.

MINI CHRISTMAS BALLS

The small red balls on the wreath are embroidered in with French knots. They are placed on every other picot, but, of course, you can make as many or as few as you like.

Work as follows:
Thread a needle with Red yarn.
Make a knot on one end.
Insert needle from WS, where one of the French knots will be placed. Tug on yarn so the knot stays firmly on the WS and can't be pulled through.

Wrap yarn around the needle tip 2–3 times.
Insert needle into same spot or directly to the side of the place where the thread first came up.
When the needle is pushed down into the spot where the yarn came up, you can carefully pull the wraps off so they lie as tightly as possible on the wreath.

Now, carefully pull the yarn through the wraps and spruce branch to make a knot. The knot should lie flat against the branch and not pop out too much.

Continue the same way until there are mini balls all over the wreath.

Cut yarn and weave in ends on WS of wall.

ROOF SURFACE

The large surface areas of the roof are worked back and forth in rows of single crochet. The pattern is worked with every other stitch as an elongated single crochet (esc). An elongated single crochet is worked just like a regular single crochet, but, instead of inserting hook under the top st loop(s), it goes into the base of the stitch on the previous row. The pattern staggers on alternate rows.

The roof is finished with both brown and white edgings. The white edgings are a part of the roof's decorative snow. Both the brown and white edgings are crocheted directly onto the roof surface.

Row 1 is worked into the loops on the back of the foundation chain. The chain stitches should be somewhat loose because the chain will draw in once it is crocheted into. If necessary, use a crochet hook a quarter or half size larger for the foundation chain.

Each row begins with ch 1 as a turning chain. Even-numbered rows = RS.

Make a total of two roof surfaces for the house.

PATTERN FOR ROOF SURFACE

With Brown, ch 34 sts—the last st is a turning ch.

Row 1: Beginning in 2nd ch from hook, work 1 sc in back loop of each ch across = 33 sts.

Row 2: 1 sc in each st across = 33 sts.

Row 3: 1 esc in 1st st, (1 sc in next st, 1 esc I next st) 16 times = 33 sts.

Row 4: 1 sc in 1st st, (1 esc in next st, 1 sc I next st) 16 times = 33 sts.

Repeat Rows 3–4 until you've worked a total of 29 rows (corresponding to 2 rows of sc and 27 pattern rows). If necessary, work extra pattern rows if the roof needs more length. The roof should be a bit smaller than the diagonal sides of the end gables before the edgings are crocheted.

Cut yarn and weave in ends on WS.

EDGINGS

The roof edgings are worked with regular single crochet on the two short sides and on the last row. They are not worked across the stiches on the foundation chain, which form the roof ridge to be sewn together later with the other roof surface of the roof ridge. So the short sides won't draw in, make stitches a bit looser than those on the long sides.

With Brown.
Row 1: Turn work so the RS points in toward you and the WS points away from you. The foundation chain should be to the right and the last row to the left.

Attach yarn with 1 sl st on the corner where the roof ridge (foundation chain) and right short sides meet.
Work 1 sc in same st as sl st.
Work 1 sc for every 2 rows (1 sc for every hole in row)—the sts should be as wide as the row is high.
In the corner, where the right short side and the long side meet, work 3 sc to round the corner.
On the long side, work 1 sc in each st to the corner.

In the corner, where the long side and the short left side meet, work 3 sc to round corner.
On the left short side, work 1 sc for every 2 rows (1 sc for each hole in the row)—the sts should be as wide as the row is high.
The last st should be placed at the base at the corner between the short left side and the roof ridge (foundation chain).

Row 2: Turn work with ch 1 and work back over the sts as for Row 1.

Change to Natural White.
Row 3: Turn work with ch 1 and work back over the sts as for Row 1.

Row 4: Turn work with ch 1 and work back over the sts as for Row 1, but, work 2 sc in the corners for a soft rounding in these spots.

Cut yarn and weave in ends on WS.

CANDY CANES

The candy canes are placed at each corner of the house so, you'll need to make four candy canes total.

Each candy cane is made in one piece.

Work 23 rounds total or the number needed to make the cane the same length as the height of the wall.

The cane is worked around in a spiral.
If necessary, use a marker (thread loop or stitch marker) to indicate the beginning/end of round.

Use Natural White.
Rnd 1: Work 6 sc around a magic ring = 6 sts.
Rnds 2–23: Work 1 sc in each st around = 6 sts.
Cut yarn, leaving an end long enough to sew the opening closed.

Cut a piece of pipe cleaner 1½" (4 cm) longer than the candy cane.
Fold in each end by ¾" (2 cm) and twist ends together with rest of pipe cleaner.
This is done so there is less chance of the pipe cleaner finding its way out through the ends of the candy cane.
Insert the pipe cleaner into the cane. Be careful so you don't snag any stitches and distort the shape. If any stitches are pulled down, pull the piece out so the candy cane is once again the right length.

Close the opening by pulling it together as follows: Thread a needle with the yarn end and insert the needle into a stitch loop from the center of the hole and outward.
Do the same with all the stitches around.
After the last stitch is caught, pull the hole together by carefully drawing in the yarn end.
Weave in end.

EMBROIDERED STRIPES

With Red.
The stripes are embroidered onto the candy cane using back stitch from bottom to top. Because the cane is crocheted in a spiral, the stripes will automatically twist around the candy cane.
Each stripe begins at the center of the base on Rnd 1 and wraps up from there. Make three stripes on each candy cane. The stripes are placed with two stitch holes between each. Each stripe ends at the center of the last round.

Cut yarn and weave in end.

Make four candy canes total, as explained above.

SNOWDRIFTS

The snowdrifts are crocheted directly onto the foundation chain. The billowing effect is made by working stitches of various lengths. All the snowdrifts are made the same way. The pattern repeat consists of 7 or 10 stitches, what are repeated on the foundation chain.

If the snowdrifts become too short in relation to the walls and roof, they can be lengthened by crocheting more chains and adding more single-crochet stitches at the end of each pattern repeat or only at each end of a whole snowdrift.

Row 1 is worked into the loops on the back of the foundation chain.

The chain stitches should be somewhat loose because the chain will draw in once it is crocheted into.

If necessary, use a crochet hook a quarter or half size larger for the foundation chain.

Each snowdrift begins in the 2nd ch from the hook.

SNOWDRIFT FOR WALLS

With Natural White, ch 41—the last st is a turning chain. Leave a yarn end on chain long enough for sewing the snowdrift to the wall.

Beginning in 2nd ch from hook, work into back of chain sts.
*In the next 10 sts, work:
1 sc, 1 hdc, 2 dc, 2 hdc, 2 dc, 1 hdc, 1 sc.*

Repeat *-* 3 more times.

Cut yarn and weave in end on WS of snowdrift.

Make a total of two snowdrifts as explained above.

SNOWDRIFT FOR END GABLE WITH A DOOR

Ch 8—the last st is a turning chain. Leave a yarn end on chain long enough for sewing the snowdrift to the wall.

In the next 7 sts, work:
1 sc, 2 hdc, 1 dc, 2 hdc, 1 sc.

Cut yarn and weave in end on WS of snowdrift.

Make a total of two snowdrifts as explained above. The drifts will be placed with one on each side of the door.

SNOWDRIFT FOR END GABLE WITH WINDOW

With Natural White, ch 28—the last st is a turning chain. Leave a yarn end on chain long enough for sewing the snowdrift to the wall.

*In the next 10 sts, work:
1 sc, 1 hdc, 2 dc, 2 hdc, 2 dc, 1 hdc, 1 sc.*

In the next 7 sts, work:
1 sc, 2 hdc, 1 dc, 2 hdc, 1 sc.

Repeat *-* in last 10 sts.

Cut yarn and weave in end on WS of snowdrift.

SNOWDRIFT FOR ROOF RIDGE

With Natural White, ch 50—the last st is a turning chain. Leave a yarn end on chain long enough for sewing the snowdrift to the roof.

Work 1 sc in 2nd ch from hook.
*In the next 10 sts, work:
1 sc, 1 hdc, 2 dc, 2 hdc, 2 dc, 1 hdc, 1 sc.*

Repeat *-* once more.

In the next 7 sts, work:
1 sc, 2 hdc, 1 dc, 2 hdc, 1 sc.

Repeat *-* 2 more times.

1 sc in last st.

Cut yarn and weave in end on WS of snowdrift.

Make 2 snowdrifts total for the roof ridge.

CHART 4—ICICLES

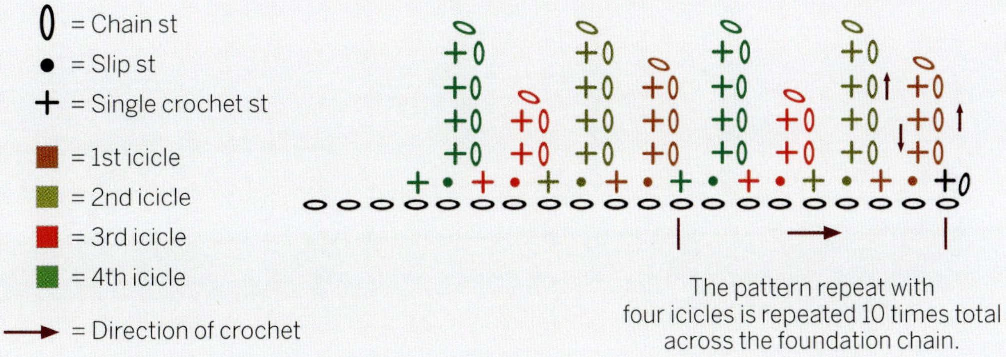

ICICLES

The icicles are crocheted directly onto the foundation chain. They are shaped with single crochet back along the foundation chain.

A pattern repeat consists of four different icicles. The pattern repeat is worked a total of 10 times per row.

Two strands of icicles are worked to hang from the roof. The strands are then attached to the two roof surfaces.

When crocheting into the chain, work into the loop on the back of the chain. This applies to both the chain sts on the foundation chain and on the icicles.

With Natural White, ch 82—the last st is a turning ch.
Work 1 sc in 2nd ch from hook.

1st Icicle:
Ch 4—the last st is a turning ch.
Beginning in 2nd ch from hook, work:
1 sc in each of the next 3 ch (3 sc total).
1 sl st into next ch of foundation chain.
1 sc into next ch of foundation chain.

2nd Icicle:
Ch 5—the last st is a turning ch.
Beginning in 2nd ch from hook, work:
1 sc in each of the next 4 ch (4 sc total).
1 sl st into next ch of foundation chain.
1 sc into next ch of foundation chain.

3rd Icicle:
Ch 3—the last st is a turning ch.
Beginning in 2nd ch from hook, work:
1 sc in each of the next 2 ch (2 sc total).
1 sl st into next ch of foundation chain.
1 sc into next ch of foundation chain.

4th Icicle:
Ch 5—the last st is a turning ch.
Beginning in 2nd ch from hook, work:
1 sc in each of the next 4 ch (4 sc total).
1 sl st into next ch of foundation chain.
1 sc into next ch of foundation chain.

Work Icicles 1–4 a total of 10 times or to end of foundation chain.

Cut yarn, leaving an end long enough to sew the icicles to the roof.
Draw yarn end through last st.

BLOCKING THE ICICLES

The icicles should be blocked into shape before they are attached to the roof.

The icicles are blocked so their tips will lean parallel to the roof of the gable ends, although the center piece is blocked horizontally across the top of the walls. At the same time, all the icicles should point down vertically, including on the diagonal sides because, otherwise, they will point out at an angle when they are attached to the roof.
Firmly pin down all the icicles and foundation chain.

Leave icicles until completely dry and, shaped as above until they will be attached to the roof.

ASSEMBLY

ATTACHING THE SNOWDRIFTS TO THE WALLS AND END GABLES

Place the snowdrifts on one of the walls so the base of the drift is flush with the base of the wall.

Begin by sewing the wall and snowdrift together along the base. For a sharp base, sew the stitches through all four stitch loops in the base of the drift and wall stitches.

Use back stitch to join the pieces, going up and down along the entire base and then along the top of the snowdrift stitches.

Cut yarn and weave in ends on WS.

STIFFENING THE WALLS AND END GABLES

Once all house's snowdrifts, windows, door, and spruce branches, mini Christmas balls, and the wreath have been attached, you can stiffen the walls with chipboard. This step will make it easy to finish your house with a sharp and uniform result.

We recommend using chipboard such as the back board of a paper pad, posterboard, heavy cardstock, or something similar.
Most cardboard becomes soft when glued and will only stiffen the walls to a very small degree. The chipboard from a pad of paper is exactly strong enough to stiffen but thin enough to cut and trim with a craft knife.

Work as follows:
Begin by drawing templates of the walls and end gables, including the windows, on plain paper. This makes it easier than correcting anything on chipboard.
The templates should reach completely down to the base of the walls so the house will be stable, but, the other sides should be ⅛"–¼" (3–5 mm) smaller than the crocheted pieces so the corners of the house can be folded in toward each other.
Draw the windows onto the templates to match their placement on the crocheted pieces.
The window frame bars can be omitted if it is too difficult to add them in. If you are drawing the bars on, they should only be a tiny bit smaller than the crocheted bars.

Cut out the templates and make sure that they match the crocheted pieces.
When the templates are the correct, draw them onto the chipboard and cut and trim as necessary.

Glue the pieces together one at a time.
Make a line of PVA craft glue on the chipboard with a brush and place the corresponding crocheted piece on top.
Add glue in any places there the pieces are not completely glued together, being especially thorough at the corners.
Carefully smooth out the crocheted pieces so every row is horizontal and doesn't bulge out at the front. Place the pieces under a press and leave until completely dry.

JOINING THE WALLS AND END GABLES

Once the walls and end gables have been stiffened, it will be easy to obtain good results when assembling the pieces. The chipboard holds the stitches in place and so you shouldn't have to fumble around when holding the pieces as you sew.

The walls are sewn together with overcast stitch in the two center stitch loops on the single crochet edgings. Place the wall with the windows, WS facing WS, against the end gable with the window. Thread a needle with the same color yarn as for the walls and begin stitching along the base of the wall in the outermost stitch at the corners.

Use the back loop (the stitch loop turned away from you) on the wall, as it is turned toward you, and the front loop (the stitch loop closest to you) on the end gable with the window, facing away from you, corresponding to the center two of the four stitch loops.

Insert the needle in from the front wall with each stitch.

Sew with overcast stitch the same way around the entire wall. At the end, cut yarn and weave in the ends on WS.

Align the end gable with the door with the already-attached wall and sew these two pieces together as for the first two walls. Finally, sew the last wall to the end gable with the door. When all four walls have been sewn together into a long row, sew on the candy canes.

ATTACHING THE CANDY CANES

Lay a candy cane directly over the seam joining two walls. The candy cane should reach all the way down to the base of the house when the house stands up.

Thread a needle with the same color yarn as for the walls and insert the needle in from the WS of the wall at the top of the seam.
Insert the needle into the top of the candy cane, behind 2 stitches of the cane, and out again.
Insert the needle down into the seam on the house and pull yarn through so the candy cane lies firmly against the seam. Sew the candy cane securely over the seam in 5–6 places from the top of the seam to the base.

Cut yarn and weave in ends on WS.

Continue the same way with two more candy canes.

ASSEMBLING THE HOUSE

Abut the last two walls and sew them together as for the previous walls. Sew on the last candy cane as before.

ASSEMBLING THE ROOF

Sew the roof surfaces together before the snowdrifts and icicles are sewn on. Finally, glue card stock on for stiffening.

Work as follows:
Lay the two roof pieces together, with WS facing WS, and the two long brown sides facing up, so the four stitch loops on the foundation chain overlap.
The sides with the white edges will be used for the icicles later in the assembly process.
Thread a needle with the same color yarn as the roof. Sew the two brown roof pieces together with overcast stitch in the two center stitch loops—corresponding to the back loops on the roof that faces you and the front loops on the roof, facing away from you.

Insert the needle in from the front roof piece with every stitch.
Stitch the same way all around the brown parts of the roof. Cut yarn and weave in ends on WS.

ATTACHING THE ICICLES

The icicles are attached along the white edge of the roof.
Lay the icicles and roof with WS facing WS. If necessary, pin them together in place.
Thread a needle with the yarn end from the icicles and begin sewing at the outermost stitch at the corner of the roof, where the white edging begins.

Use the front loop of the icicles and front loops on the roof—in both cases, there is a stitch loop that faces toward you.

For each stitch, insert the needle from the side with the icicles. Sew the same way, using overcast stitch, all across the join.
Finish by cutting the yarn and weaving in the end on WS of roof's white edge.

Attach both icicle strips and roof pieces the same way.

Crochet Tips

If any of the icicles overlap each other at the roof tips, when you fold the roof, you can lay these over each other and sew them together to hold them in place.

ATTACHING THE SNOWDRIFTS TO THE ROOF

Lay the two snowdrifts with WS facing WS, the foundation chain pointing upward, and the four stitch loops lying over each other.
Sew the snowdrifts together as for the roof pieces. Make sure you don't pull the stitches in too much.

Lay the snowdrifts on the roof along the roof ridge after the roof pieces have been seamed.
Sew the snowdrifts on securely with a couple of stitches in the middle of the snowdrift and down through the middle of the roof ridge so it won't buckle.

Next, sew the snowdrift edges securely to the roof surface along the top of the stitches so they lie firmly against the roof.
Cut yarn and weave in ends on WS.

STIFFENING THE ROOF

Cut out a paper template and then chipboard for the roof as for the house walls. The chipboard should go all the way out to the white edges, where the roof ends and the icicles begin. At the roof ridge, the chipboard should be 1⁄16"–1⁄8" (2–3 mm) shorter than the crocheted piece.

Glue the chipboard to the roof pieces as for the walls.

FINISHING THE HOUSE

Fold the roof and place it on top of the house. If the roof gapes along the end gables, you can glue or sew it with a couple of stitches on the diagonal sides of the gable.

Add a small tealight-sized LED candle inside the house to create a cozy feeling.

MUSHROOMS

Something special happens when the house is decorated in December and winter nature pours in. These small dainty mushrooms cast a particular sense of coziness over everything with their red caps and white spots. With the mini mistletoe and mini Christmas stockings, they embellish the spruce and pine branches around the house. On the Christmas tree, heaped in bowls, and used on decorations, they create a hygge feeling. The mushrooms can be various sizes if they are crocheted with varying yarn sizes and types.

Skill Level

Even though the mushrooms have small parts, they are easy to make. They are worked primarily with single crochet in the round with decreases and decreases for shaping. You'll only need techniques that might be new for some crocheters on the final step of the mushroom stem. Assembly is also relatively easy, so, this is a project that most crocheters can manage.

How to Achieve Good Results

It doesn't matter if the mushroom is a bit skewed or if it wasn't crocheted evenly, but, it is important that the stitch structure be firm, so the filling is not visible through the stitch holes. It will be easiest to crochet with cotton yarn, but the mushrooms will also work fine in wool yarn with a bit of fuzzy surface. If you make the mushrooms with wool yarn, note that the yarn is elastic and that you might tighten it a bit too much when you crochet. Try crocheting with a loose hand and leave the yarn end hanging in your left hand (if you hold the crochet hook in your right hand and vice versa if you hold the hook in your left hand) to make the stitches plumper.

Technique Videos for Mushrooms

These are the techniques: Chain stitch, slip stitch, single crochet, double crochet, front post half double crochet, magic ring, crocheting around in a spiral, crocheting in back loop, increasing, decreasing, French knot, assembly of mushroom.

MATERIALS

Yarn and Fiberfill

Organic Cotton
3 g color 35 Red (color 1) and
3 g color 01 Natural White (color 2)

Organic Wool 1
3 g color 35 Red (color 1) and
5 g color 01 Natural White (color 2)

2 g fiberfill

TOOLS

Recommended crochet hook: U.S. steel size 4 (2 mm) for Organic Cotton or U.S. C-2 (2.5 mm) for Organic Wool 1

Notions: thin leather cord for hanger, blunt tapestry needle for finishing, scissors

FINISHED MEASUREMENTS

Mushroom in Organic Cotton:
approx. 1¾" (4.5 cm) high and 1½" (4 cm) in diameter

Mushroom in Organic Wool 1:
approx. 2" (5 cm) high and 1½" (4 cm) in diameter

Gauge

33 sts × 34 rnds crocheted in rounds of single crochet with Organic Cotton and hook U.S. steel size 4 (2 mm) = 4" × 4" / 10 × 10 cm.

32 sts × 36 rnds crocheted in rounds of single crochet with Organic Wool 1 and hook U.S. size C-2 (2.5 mm) = 4" × 4" / 10 × 10 cm.

Adjust hook size to obtain correct gauge if necessary.

CONSTRUCTION

Each mushroom consists of two parts: a red mushroom cap with spots and a mushroom stalk.

Both pieces are crocheted in rounds. The mushroom cap is worked around in a spiral while the stalk is worked around in a spiral up to the gills. The rounds are each joined with a slip stitch so they will be at the same height at the end of the round as at the beginning.

Finally, the two pieces are sewn together, the stalk and cap are filled, and small French knots are embroidered on the cap for decoration.

MUSHROOM CAP

The cap is crocheted around in a spiral from the center out. If necessary, use a stitch marker to indicate the beginning/end of the round.

With color 1, Red and hook U.S. steel 4 (2 mm) for Organic Cotton or U.S. C-2 (2.5 mm) for Organic Wool 1 (or hook size necessary to achieve given gauge).

Rnd 1: Work 6 sc around a magic loop = 6 sts.

Rnd 2: (Inc) 6 times = 12 sts.

Rnd 3: (Inc, 1 sc in next st) 6 times = 18 sts.

Rnd 4: (Inc, 1 sc in each of next 2 sts) 6 times = 24 sts.

Rnd 5: (1 sc in each of next 3 sts, inc) 6 times = 30 sts.

Rnd 6: 1 sc in each of next 2 sts, (inc, 1 sc in each of next 4 sts) 5 times, 1 sc in each of next 2 sts = 36 sts.

Rnd 7: 1 sc in each st around = 36 sts.

Rnd 8: (Inc, 1 sc in each of next 5 sts) 6 times = 42 sts.

Rnds 9–11: 1 sc in each st around = 42 sts.

On the next rnd, decrease to bring the cap in a bit toward the stalk.
Rnd 12: (Dec, 1 sc in each of next 5 sts) 6 times = 36 sts.

The last st on Rnd 12 is worked as a sl st so the transition between the beginning and end of the rnd will be level.

The mushroom cap is now finished.

Cut yarn and weave in ends on WS.

MUSHROOM STALK

The stalk is crocheted around in a spiral from the center out. If necessary, use stitch marker to indicate the beginning/end of the round.

With color 2, Natural White and hook U.S. steel 4 (2 mm) for Organic Cotton or U.S. C-2 (2.5 mm) for Organic Wool 1 (or hook size necessary to achieve given gauge).

Rnd 1: Work 6 sc around a magic loop = 6 sts.

Rnd 2: (Inc) 6 times = 12 sts.

Rnd 3: (Inc, 1 sc in next st) 6 times = 18 sts.

Rnd 4: (Inc, 1 sc in each of next 5 sts) 3 times = 21 sts.

Rnd 5: (Dec, 1 sc in each of next 5 sts) 3 times = 18 sts.

Rnd 6: 1 sc in each st around = 18 sts.

Rnd 7: (Dec, 1 sc in next st) 6 times = 12 sts.

Rnds 8–9: 1 sc in each st around = 12 sts.

Rnd 10: (Inc, 1 sc in each of next 2 sts) 4 times = 16 sts.

Rnd 11: 1 sc in each st around = 16 sts.

Rnd 12: (Dec, 1 sc in each of next 2 sts) 4 times = 12 sts.

Rnd 13: 1 sc in each st around = 12 sts.
To level the transition between the rounds, work an extra sl st. The stitch is crocheted in the 1st sc on Rnd 13.

Do not cut yarn.

The mushroom stalk is now finished and the gills will be crocheted on the next round. The round is joined with 1 sl st.

Rnd 14: Ch 2 to lengthen beginning of rnd. The ch sts count as 1 dc. Work 1 dc in 1st st (the st joined with ch), 2 dc in each st around. Join rnd with 1 sl st in top of ch at beginning of rnd = 24 sts.

Begin increasing on next rnd. The increase will occur automatically when you work 1 sc at the top of a dc and then work 1 relief st around the post of the same dc.

A front post half double crochet st (fp-hdc) is worked like a regular hdc, but around a dc post to produce sts like little sausages for the mushroom gills.

A fp-hdc st is worked like a regular hdc but, instead of beginning the st at the top of a dc, the crochet hook goes from the front to the back of the dc post (see techniques video or see Abbreviations on page 26 for details).

Rnd 15: Ch 1 to lengthen beginning of rnd (in this case, the ch is not included in the stitch count).
1 sc in same st as sl st, 1 fp-hdc around ch of previous rnd, 1 fp-hdc around next dc.
Rest of rnd 15: (1 sc in top of next dc, 1 fp-hdc around same dc as sc, 1 fp-hdc around next dc) 11 times.
Join rnds with 1 sl st = 36 sts.

To finish the gills, crochet 1 rnd with regular single crochet at the top of each st:
Rnd 16: 1 sc in each st around = 36 sts.
The last st on Rnd 16 is worked as a sl st so the transition between the beginning and end of the rnd will be level.

Cut yarn and weave in ends on WS of stalk.
Fill stalk so it is firm and the filling reaches the edge of the mushroom stalk.

ASSEMBLY

Before sewing the two pieces of the mushroom together, embroider French knots at random spots on the mushroom cap.

FRENCH KNOTS

Thread a needle with Natural White yarn.
Make a knot on one end.
Insert needle from WS, where one of the knots will be placed. Tug on yarn so the knot stays firmly on the WS and can't be pulled through.

Wrap yarn around the needle tip 2–3 times.
Insert needle into same spot or directly to the side of the place where the thread first came up.
When the needle is pushed down into the spot where the yarn came up, you can carefully pull the wraps off so they lie as tightly as possible on the cap.
Now, carefully pull the yarn through the wraps and cap to make a knot. The knot should lie flat against the mushroom cap and not pop out too much.

Continue the same way until the mushroom cap has knots evenly placed all over the surface.
Cut yarn and weave in ends on WS

JOINING THE MUSHROOM PARTS

Thread a needle with Natural White yarn.
Make a knot on one end.

Insert needle into a random place on WS of stalk through the gills. Pull yarn through so the knot lies firmly in at the gills and the knot cannot be pulled through.

Place the two pieces together with WS facing WS—with the stalk turned in toward you and the cap away from you.

Go through back loops (those away from you) on the stalk and single-crochet loops on WS of cap, Rnd 12.

Sew with overcast st by inserting needle in from the mushroom stalk at every stitch.
Pull a little on the yarn after every 3–4 sts so the mushroom cap will bend a little in toward the stalk.

When an opening about ¾" (2 cm) is left, fill the mushroom with fiberfill.
The mushroom should only be filled enough to hold its shape without the gills pressing out under the mushroom cap.

Sew the last part of the opening together, adding a bit more filling before you close the opening completely.

Weave in yarn ends to WS.

HANGING LOOP

If you plan on hanging the mushrooms, add a loop to the top of each mushroom cap. A thin leather cord makes a pretty finish on a mushroom.

MINI MISTLETOE

Kissing when standing under mistletoe is a sign of love. It is a cozy Christmas tradition and the mistletoe itself is a favorite Christmas plant that decorates and enhances the Christmas home.

In this pattern, you'll find a mini version, with the branches joined into a delightful little bundle to hang on greenery and small hooks around the house. These sprigs can be shaped into little wreaths and used as napkin rings on the Christmas table.

Skill Level

The mistletoe is a quick little project with many repetitions using only a few basic stitches. Once you've crocheted a single branch, the next one is easier. If you want to shape the branches for small napkin rings, you can make the assembly easier by clamping the branches around a metal ring. The assembly does require a little patience but then the branches only need to be sewn together with back stitch, up and down in the metal ring—not a difficult technique.

How to Achieve Good Results

It Is best to crochet the branches firmly and tightly with stiff leaves so they stick out a little when assembled. If you crochet loosely, they will flap together.

Technique Videos for Mini Mistletoe

These are the techniques: Chain stitch, slip stitch, single crochet, half double crochet, double crochet, crocheting in the loop on the back of a chain stitch, twisted cord, assembling mistletoe.

MATERIALS

Yarn

Organic Cotton

Mini Mistletoe:
6 g color 36, Army Green for five branches

Wreath/napkin ring:
6 g color 36, Army Green for five branches

Small amounts of color 01, Natural White, for five berries and color 35, Red, for bow

Metal ring, 2¾" (7 cm) in diameter

TOOLS

Recommended crochet hook: U.S. steel size 4 (2 mm)

Notions: Blunt tapestry needle to weave in ends, scissors

FINISHED MEASUREMENTS

Mini mistletoe: 3¾" (9.5 cm) high and 2½" (6 cm) wide

Wreath/napkin ring: approx. 2¾" (7 cm) in diameter excluding leaves

---

Gauge

33 sts × 38 rows in single crochet worked back and forth in rows with Organic Cotton and hook U.S. steel size 4 (2 mm) = 4" × 4" / 10 × 10 cm.

Adjust hook size to obtain correct gauge if necessary.

Chart
MISTLETOE

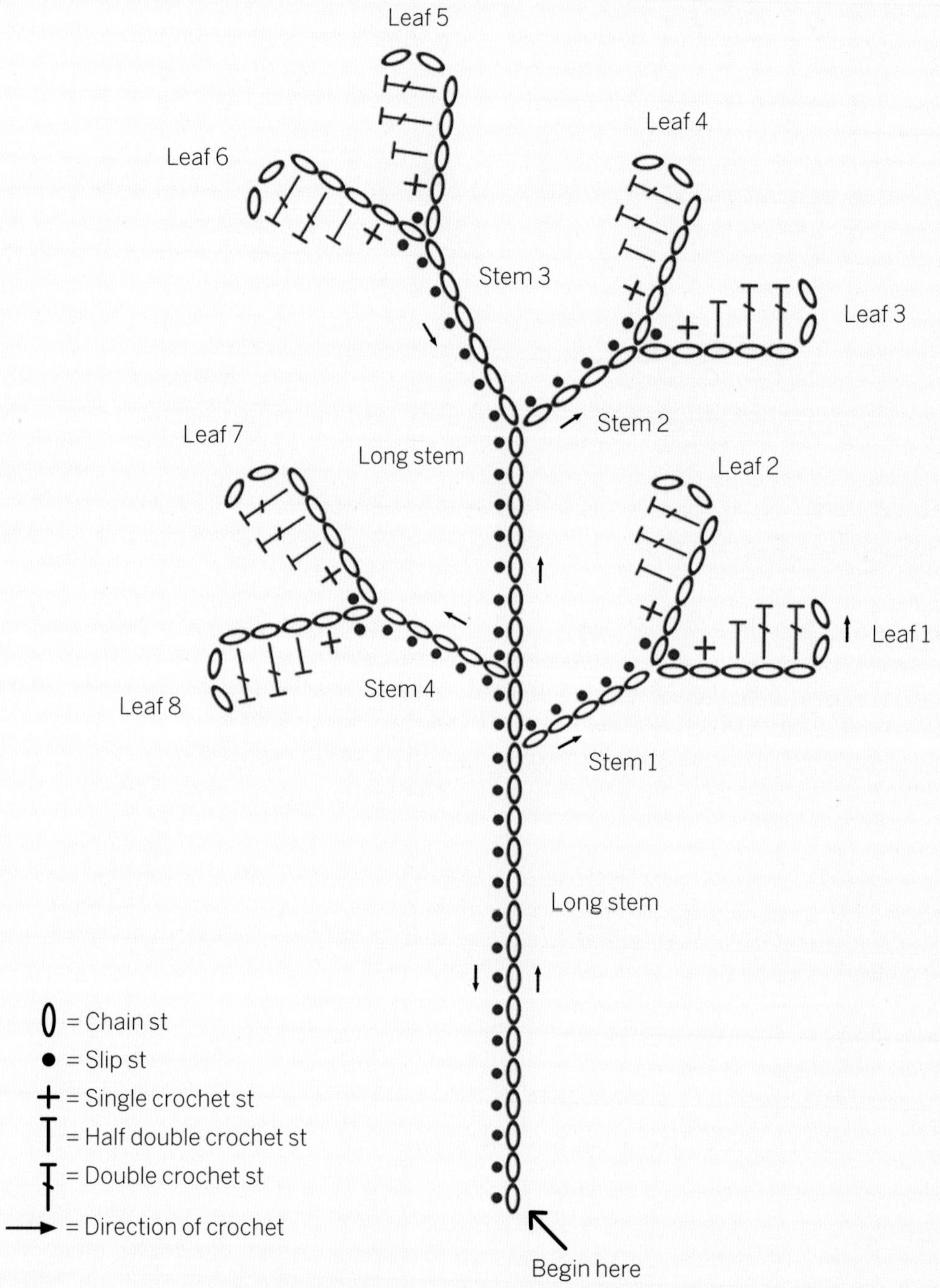

CONSTRUCTION

The mistletoe is crocheted in one piece following either the chart on the facing page or the pattern text. It begins at the base of the long stem. The small stems and leaves on the right side are crocheted at the same time as chain stitches are worked to form the mistletoe. On the way back, directly over the small stems and along the base of the long stem, you'll work slip stitches in all the chain stitches. This way, you can begin and end at the same place on the piece.

All the stitches for the stems and leaves are worked into the loops on the back of the chain stitches. This unites the top and bottom of each stitch for a smooth and even result.

The chain stitches should be worked rather loosely because they will draw in once you crochet into the chain. If necessary, use a hook one quarter or half size larger for the foundation chain. On the other hand, the chain should not be too loose or the stems and branches will not be stiff enough.

MISTLETOE

For each mistletoe, crochet five branches total. You can crochet mini berries and a small bow as decoration for the mistletoe.

WREATH/NAPKIN RING

For a wreath, crochet five branches total. Then, work a single-crochet edging around a metal ring so you can sew the branches to it.

When you crochet the branches to the napkin ring, you can omit weaving in one of the yarn ends and, instead, use for sewing the branches to the ring.

MISTLETOE BRANCH

Use Army Green and hook U.S. steel size 4 (2 mm)—or hook to obtain given gauge.

Long stem, stem 1 and leaf 1: Ch 27—the last 2 sts are the turning chain for leaf 1.

Leaf 1: 1 dc in 3rd ch from hook, 1 dc in next st, 1 hdc in next st, 1 sc in next st, 1 sl st in next st.

Leaf 2: Ch 7—the last 2 sts are the turning chain. 1 dc in 3rd ch from hook, 1 dc in next st, 1 hdc in next st, 1 sc in next st, 1 sl st in next st.

Stem 1: 1 sl st in each of next 5 sts.

Long stem, stem 2 and leaf 3: Ch 21—the last 2 sts are the turning chain for leaf 3.

Leaf 3: 1 dc in 3rd ch from hook, 1 dc in next st, hdc in next st, 1 sc in next st, 1 sl st in next st.

Leaf 4: Ch 7—the last 2 sts are the turning chain. 1 dc in 3rd ch from hook, 1 dc in next st, 1 hdc in next st, 1 sc in next st, 1 sl st in next st.

Stem 2: 1 sl st in each of next 4 sts.

Stem 3 and leaf 5: Ch 13—the last 2 sts are the turning chain for leaf 5.

Leaf 5: 1 dc in 3rd ch from hook, 1 dc in next st, 1 hdc in next st, 1 sc in next st, 1 sl st in next st.

Leaf 6: Ch 7—the last 2 sts are the turning chain. 1 dc in 3rd ch from hook, 1 dc in next st, 1 hdc in next st, 1 sc in next st, 1 sl st in next st.

Stem 3 and long stem: 1 sl st in each of next 14 sts.

Stem 4 and leaf 7: Ch 12—the last 2 sts are the turning chain for leaf 7.

Leaf 7: 1 dc in 3rd ch from hook, 1 dc in next st, 1 hdc in next st, 1 sc in next st, 1 sl st in next st.

Leaf 8: Ch 7—the last 2 sts are the turning chain. 1 dc in 3rd ch from hook, 1 dc in next st, 1 hdc in next st, 1 sc in next st, 1 sl st in next st.

Stem 4 and long stem: 1 sl st in each of next 22 sts.
Cut yarn and weave in ends.

ASSEMBLING MISTLETOE

Gather the branches into a bundle and bind them together with a strand of yarn the same color as for the branches.

If desired, crochet a bow and berries as explained below and then assemble the branches.

MINI BERRIES

Use Natural White to crochet small berries as a 2-round little balls.

Rnd 1: Work 5 sc over a magic ring = 5 sts.

Rnd 2: Work 1 sc in each st around. You can crochet into front loop only to make it easier = 5 sts.

Close rnd as follows:
Cut yarn, leaving end long enough to sew up opening.
Thread a needle with the yarn end and insert needle into front loop from center of hole and out. Do the same in each st around.
After the last st, pull hole together by tugging carefully on yarn end.

Weave in end on WS.

Make 4–5 berries as explained above and sew them securely to the branches at random spots using one strand of yarn in same color as branches.

BOW

Use Red for the bow.

The bow can either be made with a length of narrow silk ribbon or a 7" (18 cm) long chain-stitch band.

Cut yarn and weave in ends to finish cord.
Bind the cord around the branches and tie into a bow.

ASSEMBLING A WREATH/ NAPKIN RING

The small wreath has five branches, which are sewn to a metal ring with a single-crochet edging.

If necessary, use a small clamp to hold the branches onto the ring as you assemble the wreath.

Work as follows:

1. Begin by working single crochet around the metal ring. The number of single crochet stitches is not that important, but, it is important that the ring be completely covered by crochet.
2. Lay one of the branches on the ring and hold it down with small clamps.
   The first branch is sewn in the first round only at the stem. The second half should be lifted so the stem from the last branch is below.
3. Now sew the branch securely with stitches up and down through the branch and top of the stitches on the metal ring. Use the same color yarn as for the branches.
4. Lay the next branch on so the leaves overlap the stem on the first branch.
5. Sew the branch on and continue the same way all the way around the metal ring with the last branch.
6. At the last branch, lay the stem in under the stem of the first branch. Both pieces are then sewn securely on the metal ring. If they stick out too much, sew the leaves in to the metal ring with a few stitches.
7. Cut yarn and weave in ends.

DRUMS

Drums are always a part of classically traditional Christmas decor and small ones are often found hung on Christmas trees. The large drums are too big for a tree, but, on the other hand, beautiful enough to use as decoration in a window display and on a bookshelf, with their pretty colors and gold edges. The drums are lined with chipboard. The top can be removed so the box can be used as a secret space for Christmas candies or a hiding place for Advent or Christmas gifts.

Skill Level

So that the crocheted pieces of the drum will fit the paper lining, the crochet gauge must be correct for the size of the finished piece. So, you'll need some practice at crocheting evenly and uniformly for the entire project. The large drums change colors several times on a round using the Gobelin colorwork technique. Alternately, you can make a single-color tube and embroider on the lines afterward to make the project easier. The assembly takes some attention but it is not technically difficult.

How to Achieve Good Results

It is relatively easy to add or omit rounds on the white top and you can also make adjustments with more or fewer rounds and stitches on the red drum to make the crocheted pieces fit the drum box. The two-color drum is more complicated because the stitch count has to match that of the pattern repeat. For that version, it is recommended that you first crochet a gauge swatch to be certain that the frame is the right size and you won't end up with a drum tube that is too large or too small.

Technique Videos for Drums

These are the techniques: Chain stitch, slip stitch, single crochet stitch, magic ring, crocheting in the loop on the back of a chain stitch, crocheting back and forth in rows, crocheting around in a spiral, joining round with a slip stitch, attaching yarn with a slip stitch, gold edging, Gobelin color crochet, assembling a drum.

MATERIALS

Yarn and Board for Stiffening

Organic Cotton

Small drum: 27 g color 35, Red and 20 g color 01 Natural White

Large drum: 16 g color 35, Red and 41 g color 01 Natural White

Shiny Glimmergarn

Small drum: 20 g, color Gold

Large drum: 35 g, color Gold

Chipboard or Cardstock Drum Box

Small drum: 4¼" (11 cm) high and 4¼" (11 cm) in diameter

Large drum: 5¼" (13 cm) high and 5¼" (13 cm) in diameter

TOOLS

Recommended crochet hook: U.S. size C-2 (2.5 mm) for Organic Cotton and U.S. steel size 4 (2 mm) for Shiny Glimmergarn

Notions: PVA craft glue such as school glue, brush, blunt tapestry needle for assembly, scissors

FINISHED MEASUREMENTS

Small drum: approx. 4¼" (11 cm) high and 4¼" (11 cm) in diameter

Large drum: approx. 5¼" (13 cm) high and 5¼" (13 cm) in diameter

---

Gauge

32 sts × 37 rows single crochet back and forth in rows with Organic Cotton and hook U.S. size C-2 (2.5 mm) = 4" × 4" / 10 × 10 cm.

33 sts × 32 rows Gobelin colorwork single crochet back and forth in rows with Organic Cotton and hook U.S. size C-2 (2.5 mm)

Adjust hook size to obtain correct gauge if necessary.

Gauge is not important for good results with this project. Don't forget, though, that you will need more yarn if you crochet more loosely than at the gauge given above.

So that the crocheted pieces of the drum will fit the paper lining, the crochet gauge must be correct for the size of the finished piece.

CONSTRUCTION

Each drum consists of three crocheted pieces: a drum tube, crocheted back and forth in rows, a top and a base, each crocheted around in a spiral.

The small drum has a single color drum tube with decorative cords sewn on after drum assembly.

The tube for the larger drum is crocheted with two colors using Gobelin colorwork crochet.

The level of difficulty for the larger drum drops significantly if the tube is crocheted only with red yarn and the white is embroidered on with crossed stitches as shown on the chart. Note that, if you crochet the large drum only with red yarn, you'll need more red yarn than if you work with two colors.

The top and base of both drums are crocheted from the same pattern instructions to and including Round 18. The pattern stops here for the small drum but continues to Rounds 19–21 for the top and base of the large drum.
The drums are each crocheted from their specific pattern instructions but are both finished with the same techniques.

TOP AND BASE

The top and base are crocheted with color 1, Natural White. The edges are worked with Shiny Glimmergarn in color 2, Gold.

The pieces are crocheted around in a spiral. Use a marker to indicate the beginning of the round.

Begin with color 1, Natural White and hook U.S. C-2 (2.5 mm) (or hook size needed to obtain correct gauge).

Rnd 1: Work 6 sc around a magic ring = 6 sts.

Rnd 2: (Inc) 6 times = 12 sts.

Rnd 3: (Inc, 1 sc in next st) 6 times = 18 sts.

Rnd 4: (Inc, 1 sc in each of next 2 sts) 6 times = 24 sts.

Rnd 5: (1 sc in each of next 3 sts, inc) 6 times = 30 sts.

Rnd 6: 1 sc in each of next 2 sts, (inc, 1 sc in each of next 4 sts) 5 times, inc, 1 sc in each of next 2 sts = 36 sts.

Rnd 7: (Inc, 1 sc in next 5 sts) 6 times = 42 sts.

Rnd 8: 1 sc in each of next 3 sts, (inc, 1 sc in each of next 6 sts) 5 times, inc, 1 sc in each of next 3 sts = 48 sts.

Rnd 9: (1 sc in each of next 7 sts, inc) 6 times = 54 sts.

Rnd 10: 1 sc in each of next 4 sts, (inc, 1 sc in each of next 8 sts) 5 times, inc, 1 sc in each of next 4 sts = 60 sts.

Rnd 11: (Inc, 1 sc in next 9 sts) 6 times = 66 sts.

Rnd 12: 1 sc in each of next 6 sts, (inc, 1 sc in each of next 10 sts) 5 times, inc, 1 sc in each of next 4 sts = 72 sts.

Rnd 13: 1 sc in each of next 3 sts, (inc, 1 sc in each of next 11 sts) 5 times, inc, 1 sc in each of next 8 sts = 78 sts.

Rnd 14: (1 sc in next 12 sts, inc) 6 times = 84 sts.

Rnd 15: 1 sc in each of next 6 sts, (inc, 1 sc in each of next 13 sts) 5 times, inc, 1 sc in each of next 7 sts = 90 sts.

Rnd 16: 1 sc in each of next 2 sts, (inc, 1 sc in each of next 14 sts) 5 times, inc, 1 sc in each of next 12 sts = 96 sts.

Small drum Rnd 17: Inc, 1 sc in BL of each of next 15 sts around 6 times (sc in BL leaves the front loops free so you can sew on the gold edging later on) = 102 sts.

Large drum, Rnd 17: (Inc, 1 sc in each of next 15 sts) 6 times = 102 sts.

Both drums, Rnd 18: 1 sc in each of next 13 sts, (inc, 1 sc in each of next 16 sts) 5 times, inc, 1 sc in each of next 3 sts = 108 sts.

End Rnd 18 on small drum with last st as sl st to level the transition from end to beginning of rnd.

The small drum piece is now complete. Cut yarn and weave in ends. Continue to "Gold Edging."

Large drum: Continue to Rnds 19–21 below.

Rnd 19: 1 sc in each of next 4 sts, (inc, 1 sc in each of next 17 sts) 5 times, inc, 1 sc in each of next 13 sts = 114 sts.

Rnd 20: Inc, 1 sc in BL of each of next 10 sts (inc, 1 sc in BL of each of next 18 sts) 5 times, inc, 1 sc in BL of next 8 sts (sc in BL leaves the front loops free so you can sew on the gold edging later on) = 120 sts.

Rnd 21: (Inc, 1 sc in next 19 sts) 6 times = 126 sts. End Rnd 21 on large drum with last st as sl st to level the transition from end to beginning of rnd.

Cut yarn and weave in ends. Continue to "Gold Edging."

GOLD EDGING

The gold edging is crocheted directly onto the white top. In order for the gold edging to fold sharply down on the edge of lid, work Rnd 1 stitches through back loops.
The 2nd rnd is also worked through back loops, so the front loops of both rounds are free when the gold edging is finished.

Shiny Glimmergarn is somewhat thinner than Organic Cotton and so yields a different stitch structure. To produce the same stitch structure, crochet around the carried strand of Glimmergarn on the edging.

The technique is like Gobelin colorwork crochet but without any color changes.

The gold edging is crocheted in rounds. Each round is joined with 1 sl st and begun with ch 1 for some height between rounds.

The first stitch of the round is worked into the same stitch as the slip stitch. The slip stitch is not included in stitch counts.

If necessary, use a stitch marker to indicate the beginning and end of the round.

Small Drum

Use color 2, Gold.

The next rnd is worked through the back loops on the white top so the gold edging will fold down sharply on the edge of the lid.

Rnd 1: Attach yarn with 1 sl st into BL of a white st on the top.

Carry a Gold strand with the sts.

1 sc in BL in same st as sl st. 1 sc in BL of each of next 16 sts, inc in BL, (1 sc in BL of each of next 17 sts, inc in BL) 5 times = 114 sts.

Work next rnd through back loops:

Rnd 2: 1 sc in BL of each st around = 114 sts.

Rnds 3–5: 1 sc in each st around = 114 sts.

Work last st of 5th rnd as a sl st to level out the transition between beginning and end of rnd.

Measure to make sure that the gold edging covers the entire edge on the drum box. If it is too short, work an extra rnd until it is the right height.

The next round is worked through back loops so the edging will fold in over the lower edge of the lid. Do not carry an extra strand on Rnd 6.

Rnd 6: 1 sl st in BL of each st around – 114 sts. Work last st of 6th rnd as a sl st to level out the transition between beginning and end of rnd.

Cut yarn and weave in ends.

The rest of the gold edging will be crocheted when the top is attached to the drum box.

Make a top and a base for each drum.

Large Drum

Rnd 1: With color 2, Gold, attach yarn with 1 sl st into BL of a white st on the top.

Carry a Gold strand with the sts.

1 sc in BL in same st as sl st. 1 sc in BL of each of next 19 sts, inc in BL, (1 sc in BL of each of next 20 sts, inc in BL) 5 times = 132 sts.

Work next rnd through back loops:

Rnd 2: 1 sc in BL of each st around = 132 sts.

Rnds 3–8: 1 sc in each st around = 132 sts.

Measure to make sure that the gold edging covers the entire edge on the drum box. If it is too short, work an extra rnd until it is the right height.

Note The next round is worked through back loops so the edging will fold in over the lower edge of the lid.

Do not carry an extra strand on Rnd 10.

Rnd 10: 1 sl st in BL of each st around = 132 sts. Work last st of 10th rnd as a sl st to level out the transition between beginning and end of rnd.

Cut yarn and weave in ends.

The rest of the gold edging will be crocheted when the top is attached to the drum box.

Make a top and a base for each drum.

DRUM TUBE

The drum rube is worked back and forth in single-crochet rows. Begin each row with ch 1 as a turning st.

Row 1 is worked into the loops on back of the foundation chain to unite the stitch structures of the top and base with that of the crocheted drum box. The foundation chain should be crocheted somewhat loosely as it will draw in when you crochet into it. If necessary, use a hook a quarter or half size larger for the foundation chain.

The drum tubes are crocheted ⅜" (1 cm) shorter than the circumference of the drum box. When it's time to glue the crocheted pieces, it will expand and can be stretched. This also applies to the height.

Measure the piece once you've worked 6–8 rows. At that point, you should have a good idea about what the finished size will be.

SMALL DRUM

With color 3, Red and hook U.S. C-2 (2.5 mm) (or hook size to obtain given gauge), ch 97 sts—the last st is a turning ch.
Make sure the ch sts are neither too loose nor too tight—they should have the same width as a sc.

Row 1 is on WS of work.
Row 1: Beginning in 2nd ch from hook, work 1 sc in each loop on back of foundation chain—96 sts.

Rows 2–30: 1 sc in each st across = 96 sts.
If the crocheted drum tube is not the correct height in relation to the drum box, you should either omit or add more rows.
Cut yarn and weave in ends on WS.

LARGE DRUM

The large drum is crocheted in two colors following the pattern chart on the next page. One block on the chart is = 1 sc.

The drum is worked in Gobelin colorwork crochet, which encases the color not in use.

Crochet gauge changes when you work in the Gobelin technique. The stitches are lengthened so you won't crochet as many rows as for the small drum.
Note that the stitch structure is not very elastic, so, you need to measure the gauge as you work to make sure that the finished piece will fit the circumference of the drum box. The drum tube should be a bit shorter than the circumference of the drum box, but, in that case, it is better to crochet somewhat more loosely than the given gauger than to crochet more tightly. If the drum tube is even just a few millimeters too small, it might be difficult to cover the entire cardboard tube during assembly.

Row 1 is worked into the loops on back of the foundation chain. The foundation chain should be crocheted somewhat loosely as it will draw in when you crochet into it. If necessary, use a hook a quarter or half size larger for the foundation chain.

Either side of the crocheted drum tube can be considered as the RS because the joins at the color changes will be covered by the decorative cords.

Note When changing colors, joins will appear at the sides of the color change, just as you would be able to perceive the other color through the stitches. The joins (small notches) cannot be avoided because it is just how the stitches are when crocheting color changes back and forth in rows.

With color 3, Red and hook U.S. C-2 (2.5 mm) (or hook size to obtain given gauge), ch 120 sts —the last st is a turning ch.
Make sure the ch sts are neither too loose nor too tight—they should have the same width as a sc.

Turn each row with ch 1.
Row 1: Beginning in 2nd ch from hook, work 1 sc in each loop on back of foundation chain—119 sts.

Rows 2–25: 1 sc in each st across, in colors as shown on the chart to the right = 119 sts.

Work last row only with color 1, Natural White.
Row 26: 1 sc in each st across = 119 sts.

Cut yarn and weave in ends on WS.

Crochet Tips

If the crocheted drum tube is a bit too short for the drum box, work Row 26 once more to add some length. This is not shown on the chart.

CHART—DRUM TUBE

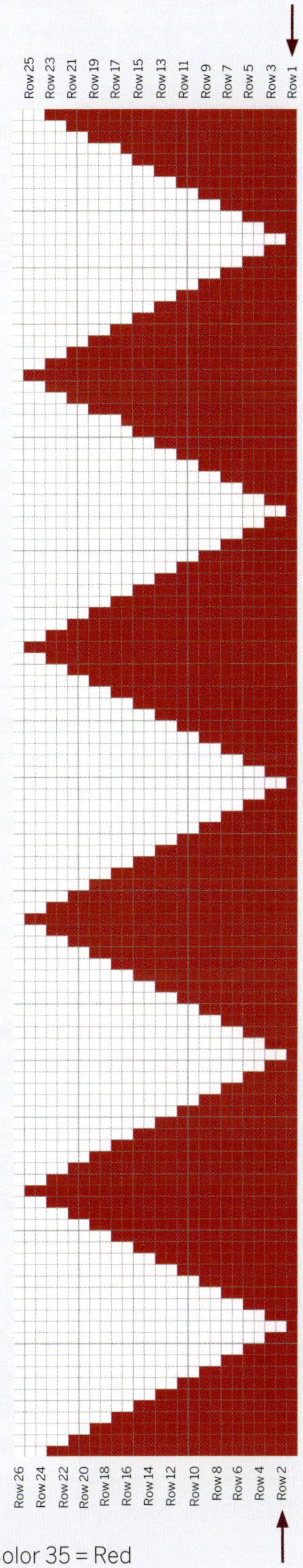

■ = Color 35 = Red

□ = Color 1 = Natural White

← = Read chart from right to left = on WS.

→ = Read chart from left to right = on RS

Crochet Tips

If the crocheted piece is a bit too short, you can work an extra row for more width on the tube. This will keep you from have to begin all over again.

SINGLE CROCHET ALONG THE SHORT SIDES

To make the sides of the drum tube more stable, work single crochet on the short sides. This will make it easier to achieve a uniform and even result when seaming the sides.
The single-crochet edges are worked on the right side of the short sides. The single-crochet edges from the base and up and, on the left side, from the top down.
The number of stitches depends on how the stitches are placed and how tightly they are worked. As a starting point, work 1 sc in each row at the same time, skipping every 5th row.

The edging should neither ruffle nor draw in. If the single-crochet edging ruffles, there are too many stitches. If the edge draws in, there are too few stitches. At the same time, it is important, to have the same number of stitches at each side because you will use them for seaming the sides.

Work as follows:
Use color 3, Red for both drums.
Attach yarn with 1 sl st in a corner of the short side on the drum tube. Work 1 sc in same st as sl st.
Continue, working sc along the entire side.
When you've worked sc all along the edge, cut the yarn and weave in the ends on WS.

ASSEMBLY OF TOP AND BASE

Glue the crocheted pieces on the drum box. We recommend using a PVA craft glue that won't dry too quickly. It should be possible to arrange the crocheted pieces into place and move them as needed. School glue is easy to work with because it is mild, doesn't have an after-smell, and dries slowly.

Work as follows:

1. Find the center of the card stock on the lid and mark it with a small dot. Draw glue across the top of the lid—avoid the edges to begin with. Use a brush to make a smooth and even layer of glue.
2. Fold the crocheted gold edging up on the white crocheted piece.
3. Stick a pin through the center of the crocheted top and set the pin down in the center of the lid.
4. Smooth the white piece and push it into place. Fold the gold edging down around the edge of the lid and, finally, move the white part into place.
5. Let the glue dry completely before the gold edging is glued.
6. Fold the gold edging up and away from the edge.
7. Brush glue onto the edge of the card stock lid—and also the little piece that bends in toward the tube. Brush on a smooth and even layer of glue.

8. Pull the gold edging down and, finally, move it into place. Be careful that the last round with slip stitches lite on the little edge where it bows in toward the drum tube.
9. Let the glue dry completely.
10. Glue the base on the same way.

FINISHING THE GOLD EDGINGS

The gold edgings folded in over the top or base of the lid are finished being crocheted when the top/base is attached to the drum box. It is a little more difficult to crochet while you hold onto the card stock pieces but it will make the final assembly much easier.

Crochet around. Join each rnd with 1 sl st to level the round.
The 1st st of the rnd is worked in the same st as for the sl st. The sl st is not included in the stitch counts.

If necessary, use a stitch marker to indicate the beginning and end of the rnd.

Crochet Tips

This step can be omitted on the drum base and worked only on the drum lid if you prefer. It makes a lower base that stands more sharply and is less visible.

Instead of following the instructions below for the drum base, you can crochet a round of slip stitches for Rnd 1.

Small Drum

Use color 2, Gold.
Rnd 1: Place the piece so the top of the lid points upward and the gold edging points down.

Attach yarn with 1 sl st to a free st loop in Gold from the 2nd rnd and the free stitch loop in White cotton on the 1st rnd.

Add a Gold strand to carry along behind the stitches.

Work 1 sc in same st as sl st and then 1 sc in each st around. End rnd with 1 sl st = 114 sts.

Rnd 2: (Dec in BL, 1 sc in BL of each of next 17 sts) 6 times. End rnd with 1 sl st = 108 sts.

Rnd 3: (Dec, 1 sc in each of next 16 sts) 6 times. End rnd with 1 sl st = 102 sts.
Work last st of Rnd 3 as a sl st to level transition between beginning and end of rnd.

Cut yarn, leaving an end long enough to use for sewing gold edging to white lid.

Large Drum

Use color 2, Gold.
Rnd 1: Place the piece so the top of the lid points upward and the gold edging points down.

Attach yarn with 1 sl st to a free st loop in Gold from the 2nd rnd and the free stitch loop in White Cotton on the 1st rnd.

Add a Gold strand to carry along behind the stitches.
Work 1 sc in same st as sl st and then 1 sc in each st around. End rnd with 1 sl st = 132 sts.

Work in back lops on next round.
Rnd 2: (Dec in BL, 1 sc in BL of each of next 20 sts) 6 times. End rnd with 1 sl st = 126 sts.

Rnd 3: (Dec, 1 sc in each of next 19 sts) 6 times. End rnd with 1 sl st = 120 sts.
Work last st of Rnd 3 as a sl st to level transition between beginning and end of rnd.

Cut yarn, leaving an end long enough to use for sewing gold edging to white lid.

Sewing Top On

When sewing the gold edging to the white crocheted piece, if can be a bit difficult to hold all the pieces in place. The technique itself is not difficult, but, there are many pieces to be held in place without getting the lid squashed.
A curved needle will make it easier, but, it is also possible to use a regular blunt-tipped needle.

Put the lid on the drum tube and set it all on a table in front of you to make the sewing easier.

Work as follows:

1. Insert needle under both stitch loops on the gold edging (out from the drum edge and in toward the center) and in under the free stitch loop on the white crocheted top.
2. Sew back under the same gold stitch loop (from the center of the drum lid and out to the edge of the drum).
3. Go to the next gold stitch and repeat steps 1–2. Continue the same way all the way around.

Do not tighten the yarn so much that the white stitch loop is drawn in through the gold edging. The two pieces should just meet each other.

If the gold edging has more stitches than the round with the free stitch loops, or if the stitches are staggered in relation to each other, you can fix it by decreasing evenly spaced over the gold sts of the rnd. Insert the hook in under the same stitch loop of step 1 when the next gold stitch is sewn.

Weave in ends under fold of gold edging on the lid.

ASSEMBLING DRUM TUBE

The crocheted drum tube is glued onto the drum box and then sewn together along the short sides.

When the crocheted part is wet with glue, it can be stretched a little in both width and length.

Work as follows:

1. Brush glue onto a smaller piece of the paper tube where the center of the crocheted piece will be placed. Smooth it out in an even layer with a brush.
2. Place the crocheted piece on top and smooth it out so it sits precisely in the center of the height and the row ridges are horizontal.
3. Glue the rest of the paper tube and then use a brush to smooth it into an even layer.

4. Smooth out the rest of the crocheted piece and pull the ends as tightly to each other as possible. There should be only a maximum of 1⁄16" (a couple of millimeters) space between them.
5. Let glue dry completely.

SEAMING THE ENDS

Seam the ends of the drum tube together with overcast stitch into the two top stitch loops on the crocheted piece by inserting the needle in from the same side on every stitch.
Weave in ends on WS.

CROSSHATCHING ("HARLEQUINS") ON THE SMALL DRUM

Make the crosshatching for the small drum with White yarn. You will have 10 "harlequins" around the drum.
If there are no natural spots for positioning the crosses as on the large drum, mark the top and base of each harlequin with a pin, before making the crosses.

The crosses are made over two rounds.

Work as follows:

1. Place five pins evenly spaced in the top stitches of the crocheted drum tube. Since there are 96 stitches total from the join, there should be 19–20 sts between each pin. The first pin is placed at the center of the seam on the ends.
2. Now place pins on the base of the crocheted drum tube, staggered below the top pins so they sit centered between the top pins.
3. Make a knot on one end of an approx. 43¼" (110 cm) long strand of yarn.
4. Insert strand so the knot sits firmly on the WS, behind the seam.
5. Now zigzag alternately from the top to the base of the tube. The yarn should be stitched in behind the front loops. For an especially nice cord, pull the yarn behind the attached cord, before continuing to the next spot.
6. Continue the same way around until there are a total of five triangles.
7. Repeat steps 1–6 in mirror-image on the drum tube by placing ten new pins at the center of the base of each triangle. The yarn twists and is not sewn opposite for making five new triangles, upside down from the first five triangles. This way, the triangles become ten harlequins.
8. Weave in ends on WS.

SEAMING THE ENDS

Seam the ends of the drum tube using overcast stitch in the two top stitch loops of the crocheted piece by inserting needle in from the same side of each stitch.

Crochet Tips

If sewing the seams isn't for you, you can glue the gold edging to the white top instead.

CROSSHATCHING ON THE LARGE DRUM

On the large drum, you can make the decorative cords along the triangles with crocheted chains. The cords will cover the small hashmarks where the color changes were made and make the triangles stand out sharply.

Either side of the drum tube can be used as the right side. Choose the side where the cords will lie most smoothly and cover as much as possible of the hashmarks.

Ch 40 or the number of stitches to match the length of the teeth and diagonally over the teeth from the top of the drum tube to the base. Leave an end on the chain long enough for sewing on the chain.

Cut yarn with an end 9¾" (25 cm) long and pull the end through the last chain.

Sew the chain on as follows:
Thread needle with yarn end from chain.

Lay the chain on one tooth, at the same time leaving 1 ch abutting the edge of the drum tube. Insert needle in from WS of tube in the top of the st where the chain will begin out from. Now insert the needle in the first st on back of chain. Tighten so the st and yarn lie completely flush at the edge of the tube.
Sew another st the same way.

Thread the needle with the other yarn end and sew the same way on the other end of the chain securely to the top of the drum edge. (If there are too many ch sts, you can undo some before the chain is completely sewn on.)

Now sew with back st up and down in the center of the chain, down along the chain in 4–5 spots.

Make a couple of sts at the other end the same way.

Weave in ends on WS.

MOR

GINGERBREAD HEARTS

These gingerbread hearts are a true classic Christmas cookie. For our crocheted version, a pretty decoration for the Christmas tree, the lace glimmers among the Christmas lights. You can make some for the Christmas table to use as place cards with embroidered names, and they make for especially personal little gifts if used as to / from cards. The hearts are lovely on their own and can be crocheted in any Christmas color and embellished with a ribbon hanging loop.

Skill Level

The hearts are a good project to begin with if you don't have much crochet experience. They are charming and can be even more individual if they are not perfectly shaped. The hearts are also pretty in other colors. To make it easier, make the first heart without any embroidery or lace.

How to Achieve Good Results

Be careful to crochet evenly and firmly so the filling won't be visible through the stitch holes when the pieces are sewn together. The shape of the heart will be more uniform and symmetrical if the individual pieces are blocked before assembly. The striped cord or another pretty loop gives the hearts just the right look.

Technique Videos for Gingerbread Hearts

These are the techniques: Chain stitch, single-crochet stitch, crocheting back and forth in rows, crocheting in the loop on the back of a chain stitch, increasing, decreasing, attaching yarn with a slip stitch, crocheted lace, embroidered cross stitch, embroidered back stitch, twisted cord, assembling the heart.

MATERIALS

Yarn and Fiberfill

Organic Cotton
14 g color 30, Brown
Small amounts color 01, Natural White and color 35, Red for twisted cord

Shiny Glimmergarn
3–4 g color Mother-of-Pearl

3–5 g fiberfill

Optional: ribbon for hanging loop

TOOLS

Recommended crochet hook: U.S. steel size 4 (2 mm) for Organic Cotton and or U.S. steel size 5 (1.75 mm) for Shiny Glimmergarn

Notions: Blunt tapestry needle to weave in ends, scissors

FINISHED MEASUREMENTS

Approx. 3½" (9 cm) long and 4" (10 cm) wide before seaming

Gauge

38 sts × 40 rows of single crochet worked back and forth in rows with hook U.S. steel size 4 (2 mm) = 4" × 4" / 10 × 10 cm.

Adjust hook size to obtain correct gauge if necessary.

The hearts can easily be crocheted a bit more loosely than at the given gauge. As long as the stitch structure is firm, your gauge can differ somewhat, although the size of the finished heart and yarn amount needed will differ.

Chart
GINGERBREAD HEART

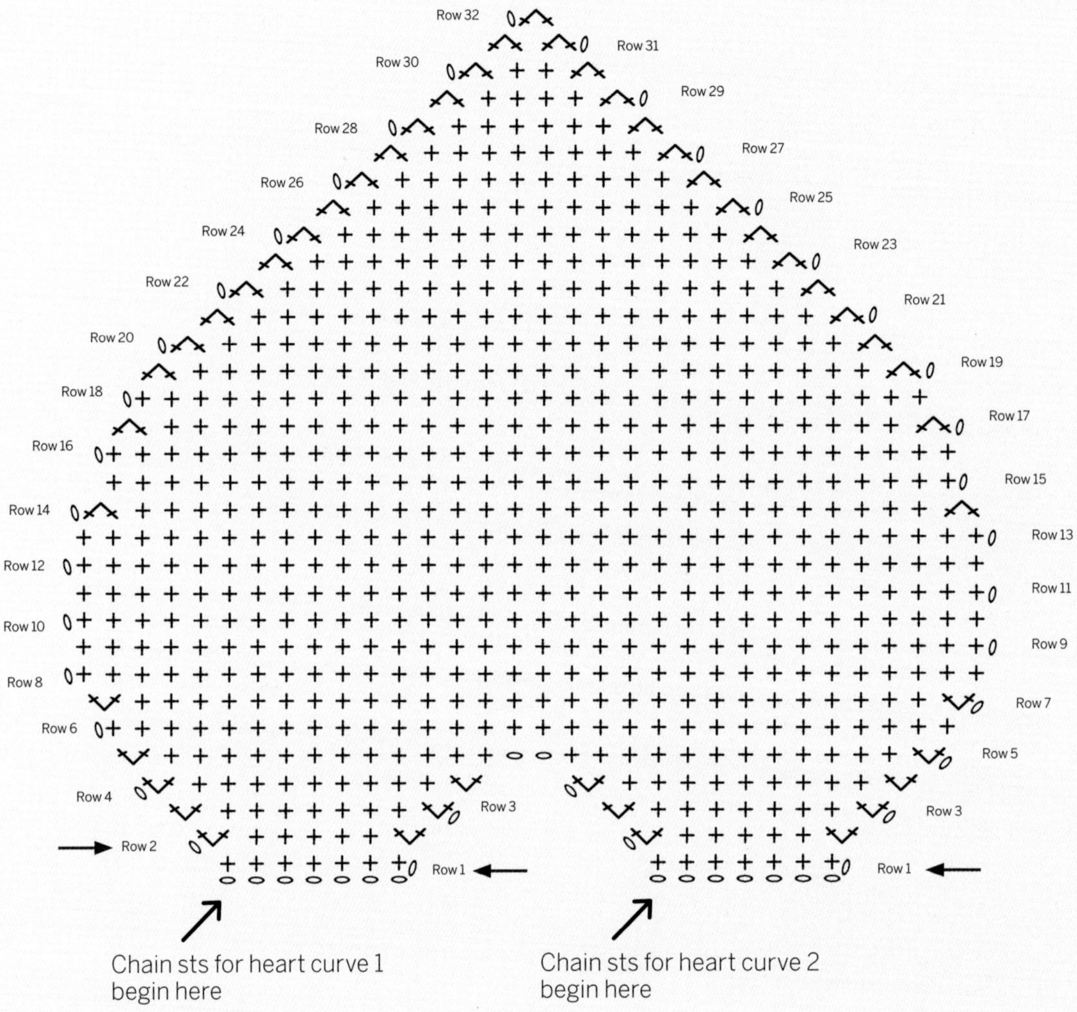

0 = Chain stitch (ch st)

+ = Single crochet stitch (sc)

= 2 sc in same st = increase (inc)

= skip 1 st, 1 sc in next st (sk-dec)

← = Direction of crochet

CONSTRUCTION

The gingerbread heart consists of two individual pieces, with each crocheted back and forth in rows.

Each piece is worked from the curves of the heart and down to the tip. The curves are each crocheted separately for the first 4 rows and then joined on the 5th row.

The piece finishes with a single-crochet edging all the way around the heart.

The fine lace is crocheted separately and sewn onto the heart before the two heart pieces are sewn together.
It is recommended that you also embroider the heart pieces before they are sewn together because it is easier to weave in the ends and you'll avoid having the filling pulled out through the stitch holes.

Finally, attach a ribbon or cord for hanging the heart.

Row 1 is worked into the loops on back of the piece. The top and bottom of the stitches are therefore united and the heart curves will be stable at the top. It is easier to crochet the single-crochet edging around the heart last.
When Row 1 is crocheted into the loops on the back of the chain stitches, the chain stitches should be a bit loose because they will draw in once you crochet into them. If necessary, use a hook a quarter or half size larger for the foundation chain.

All the even-numbered rows are on the RS, which will be important when you crochet the heart curves together.

Turn every row with ch 1 as a turning ch.

HEART CURVE

Use hook U.S. steel 4 (2 mm) or size hook necessary to obtain gauge.
Ch 8—the last st is a turning ch.

Row 1: Beginning in 2nd ch from hook, work 1 sc in loop on back of each ch on foundation chain = 7 sts.

Row 2: Inc, 1 sc in each of next 5 sts, inc = 9 sts.

Row 3: Inc, 1 sc in each of next 7 sts, inc = 11 sts.

Row 4: Inc, 1 sc in each of next 9 sts, inc = 13 sts.

Cut yarn and weave in ends.

Make another heart curve with 4 rows as above, but, do not cut yarn. Continue to next row.

On the next row, join the two pieces:
Row 5: Inc, 1 sc in each of next 12 sts, ch 2.
Hold the first heart curve with the WS facing you—you will continue with Row 5 as for first curve with 1 sc in the first st on the next curve, 1 sc in each of next 11 sts, inc = 30 sts.

REST OF HEART

On the next row, you'll crochet over the sts on both heart curves as well as through the 2 ch sts between the heart curves. It is important to crochet through the ch sts and not around them because the ch sts will also be used for the single-crochet edging.

Row 6: 1 sc in each of next 14 sts, 1 sc in each ch, 1 sc in each of next 14 sts = 30 sts.

Row 7: Inc, 1 sc in each of next 28 sts, inc = 32 sts.

Rows 8–13: 1 sc in each st across = 32 sts.

On the next row, you'll begin decreasing to shape the tip of the heart. Decrease by skipping 1 st each at the beginning and end of the row. Be careful not to work too tightly when decreasing; if you do the edging will draw in.

Row 14: Sk-dec, 1 sc in each of next 28 sts, sk-dec = 30 sts.

Rows 15–16: 1 sc in each st across = 30 sts.

Row 17: Sk-dec, 1 sc in each of next 26 sts, sk-dec = 28 sts.

Row 18: 1 sc in each st across = 28 sts.

Row 19: Sk-dec, 1 sc in each of next 24 sts, sk-dec = 26 sts.

Row 20: Sk-dec, 1 sc in each of next 22 sts, sk-dec = 24 sts.

Row 21: Sk-dec, 1 sc in each of next 20 sts, sk-dec = 22 sts.

Row 22: Sk-dec, 1 sc in each of next 18 sts, sk-dec = 20 sts.

Row 23: Sk-dec, 1 sc in each of next 16 sts, sk-dec = 18 sts.

Row 24: Sk-dec, 1 sc in each of next 14 sts, sk-dec = 16 sts.

Row 25: Sk-dec, 1 sc in each of next 12 sts, sk-dec = 14 sts.

Row 26: Sk-dec, 1 sc in each of next 10 sts, sk-dec = 12 sts.

Row 27: Sk-dec, 1 sc in each of next 8 sts, sk-dec = 10 sts.

Row 28: Sk-dec, 1 sc in each of next 6 sts, sk-dec = 8 sts.

Row 29: Sk-dec, 1 sc in each of next 4 sts, sk-dec = 6 sts.

Row 30: Sk-dec, 1 sc in each of next 2 sts, sk-dec = 4 sts.

Row 31: (Sk-dec) 2 times = 2 sts.

Row 32: Sk-dec = 1 st.

Do not cut yarn. Continue to section "Single-Crochet Edging."

SINGLE-CROCHET EDGING

To join the two pieces of the heart evenly, make a single-crochet edging around the entire heart.

Be very careful not to crochet tightly when working the single crochet because then the edges will pull in. If you need to crochet more loosely, use a hook a quarter or half size larger.

The number of stitches to be crocheted depends on where you insert the hook and how close the stitches are. The main point is that the heart pieces should not ruffle or pull in nor should they change shape. This especially applies to the long diagonal sides at the tip of the heart.
If the heart edges ruffle, there are too many stitches; if the edges pull in, there are too few stitches.

It is important to place the stitches at approximately the same spot on each of the two heart pieces so you can work the seam evenly.

On top of the heart curve, you will work 1 sc in each of the 7 sc on row 1.

At the curves and corners, work 2 sc to round the corner. Alternately, you can crochet the stitches more loosely at these places, so the top of these stitches will be longer and more elastic over a longer piece.

At the base of the heart curve, you can add a single sc so the stitches won't clump together. When the single-crochet edging has been worked all the way around the heart, cut the yarn and weave in the ends.

LACE

This lace is a somewhat simplified version of a crocheted picot edging. It is worked directly onto a foundation chain so it will be as thin as possible.

You can stretch the lace out a little so we recommend making it a bit shorter than the heart. If the lace is too short, you can place it further in on the heart where it doesn't need to be as long as for all the way around the outer edge of the heart.

The pattern repeat is a multiple of 2. If the lace needs to be longer, add 2 more stitches for an extra picot. If the lace needs to be shorter, remove 2 sts for each picot removed.

Note All the picots are crocheted in the loops on back of the foundation chain as for the beginning of the heart curves.

Ch 91—the last 2 sts are the turning ch.

First picot on row:
1 sl st in 2nd loop from hook.
1 sl st in next loop.
Skip 1 loop.
1 sl st in next loop.

The first picot will be a little differently shaped than the others, but it adjusts once the lace is sewn onto the heart.

Rest of the picots:
Ch 2, 1 sl st in 2nd ch from hook.
Slip 1 ch.
1 sl st in next ch.

Repeat the picots across rest of foundation chain for about 44 picots total.

Cut yarn, leaving an end long enough for sewing lace to heart.

Weave in ends from foundation chain on back of lace.

SEWING ON LACE

Lay the lace on the heart, making sure that one picot tip is placed at the tip of the base of the heart and one at the top where the heart curves meet. Place the base of the lace about ⅜" (1 cm) in from the edge of the heart.

If you are not going to embroider on the heart, the lace can be placed a little further in. In this case, the lace edge can be ½" (1.25 cm) in from the edge of the heart.

Pin the lace securely into place.

Thread a needle with the yarn end, make a stitch right over the picot top—the stitch is placed from the base (at the chain st) and up to the tip of the picot top.

Sew the same way over each lace picot.

When the last picot has been sewn down, pull it over to the first picot top of the round to close up the space between the beginning and end.

Weave in ends on WS of heart and cut yarn.

CHART—LACE

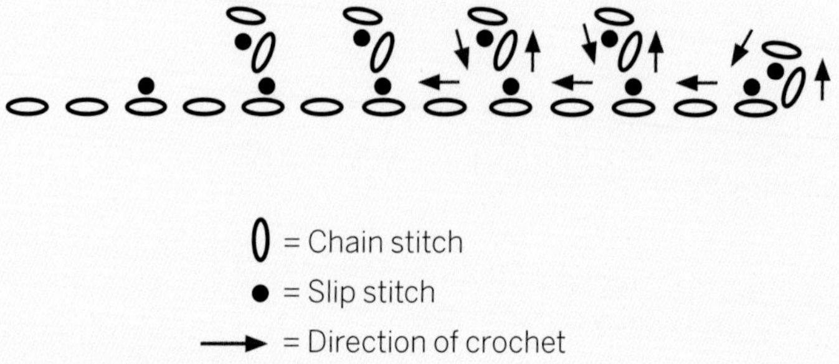

EMBROIDERY

The gingerbread hearts will be especially beautiful with a little embroidery. The embroidery can be anything from small snowflakes to names and letters.

The embroidery shown in the photos can be embroidered freehand or in cross stitch. You can use a few more letters with freehand embroidery because the stitches take less space than for cross stitch.

You can draw your own pattern on graph paper or use the cross stitch pattern below.

We used Shiny Glimmergarn and Organic Cotton for the embroidery in the pictures.

The embroidered motifs should be centered on the heart, in both width and length.

The cross stitch embroidery on the heart is placed over Rows 11–18 as counted from the top down.

The freehand embroidery with the text "mor" (mother) on the heart is placed over Rows 13–18 as counted from the top down.

CHART—EMBROIDERY

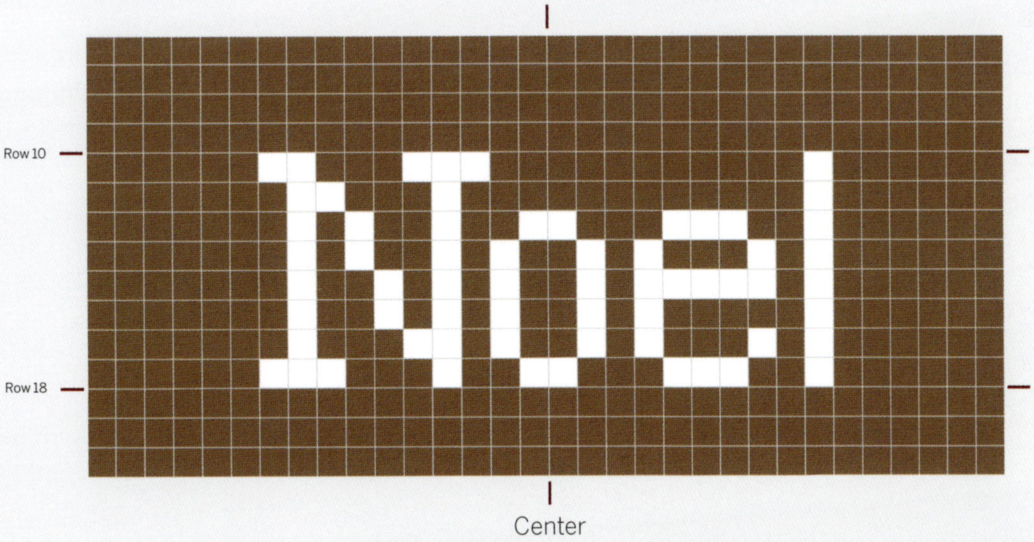

■ = Color 30, Brown

□ = Color 01, Natural White

1 square on the chart = 1 cross stitch

The stitch is embroidered in the color shown on the chart.

Cross stitches are worked over 4 holes on the crocheted area.
The 4 holes correspond to the holes around one crocheted stitch.
Weave in all ends on WS of piece.

ASSEMBLY

You will achieve a truly lovely and uniform result if you block the pieces before you assemble them. Begin by blocking the heart pieces and lace as explained on page 25.

The two heart pieces are sewn together with overcast stitch in the two center stitch loops of the single-crochet edges.

Lay the two heart pieces together with WS facing WS—with RS of single-crochet edging outward on each piece.
Begin seaming at one end of the long sides of the heart.

Use the BL (the stitch loop away from you) on the heart piece that is turned in toward you and the FL (the stitch loop closest to you) on the heart piece that is turned away from you.

Insert needle in from the front heart piece with every stitch.

When an opening of about ¾" (2 cm) remains, fill the heart with fiberfill. There should be about 4–5 g fiberfill in the heart, depending on how full you want it. The heart will be flat, but, at the same time, look a bit full like a real gingerbread heart.

Sew the last part of the heart together, inserting a bit more fiberfill before you close it up entirely.

Cut yarn and weave in ends.

TWISTED TWO-COLOR CORD

The classic two-color cord adds a pretty touch with the colors twisted around each other.

Work as follows:

Cut two strands 59" (1.5 m) long in two different colors. Fold each strand at the middle to double it.

Join the two strands together at one end so they hang together at the center with a knot and become one long cord.

The strands of color 1 can be held, for example, on a doorknob, while you hold the color 2 strands in you hand. You might also attach the end to a pencil to make it easier to hold.

Stretch the strands out so they tighten and the knot is at the center of the cord.

Begin by twisting the entire cord so it twists on itself 50–100 times, depending on how tight you want the twists. The more times you twist it around, the tighter the cord will be.

Fold the cord at the center (at the knot) so the two ends meet. It will help to hold one finger on the knot as you continue to stretch the strands out completely so they don't twist together at unintended places.

The strands will now twist up on themselves and make a two-color cord. Knot the ends together so they don't keep twisting.

Draw the cord through the heart and join the ends.

Noel

MINI CHRISTMAS STOCKINGS

It's not easy to put gifts in these mini Christmas stockings, but they are enormously sweet hanging on branches with crocheted mushrooms and mini mistletoe. They can also be used to decorate and personalize Christmas gifts. You can make them in any colors you like with different color stripes; single-color and embroidered with dots and letters; or, they'll be ever so pretty in classic red and white.

Skill Level

The Christmas stockings are totally easy because they are crocheted around in a spiral throughout with only a few increases. However, the skill level is considered as intermediate because of the division for leg and heel. At that point, you'll use techniques you might not have tried previously. As soon as you get the concept of the heel turn, the Christmas stockings will be easy.

How to Achieve Good Results

Wool is elastic and you can easily stretch it too much when crocheting. As it happens, the Christmas stockings should have a rather firm structure. Try to crochet with a somewhat loose hand, with the yarn end hanging loose in your left hand (if you hold the hook in your right hand and vice versa if you hold the hook in your left hand). This will leave the wool soft and airy in structure and make the stockings a bit slack while looking stiff.

Technique Videos for Christmas Stockings

These are the techniques: Chain stitch, single-crochet stitch, double crochet, magic ring, crocheting around in a spiral, increasing, joining a round with slip stitch, color changes, attaching yarn to a stitch loop,dividing for leg and heel.

MATERIALS

Yarn and Hanging Cord

Organic Wool 1
3 g color 35, Red and
5 g color 01, Natural White

OR

Organic Cotton
3 g color 35, Red and
5 g color 01, Natural White

Thin leather cord for hanging

TOOLS

Recommended crochet hook: U.S. size D-3 (3 mm)

Notions: Blunt tapestry needle to weave in ends, scissors

FINISHED MEASUREMENTS

The Christmas stockings are about 2½" (6 cm) long and 1¼" (3 cm) wide

---

Gauge

32 sts × 36 rnds crocheted in single crochet st with Organic Wool 1 and hook U.S. size D-3 (3 mm) = 4" × 4" / 10 × 10 cm.

Adjust hook size to obtain correct gauge if necessary.

The Christmas stockings are so small that it doesn't matter what you use for yarn if the stockings are crocheted at a looser gauge than given above.

CONSTRUCTION

The Christmas stocking is crocheted around in one piece using Organic Wool 1 or Organic Cotton. The stocking is worked in three parts:
The first part begins at the toe and continues up the foot. For the second part, you'll divide the piece for leg and heel with a chain stitch loop across. On the right side of the piece (if you have the hook in your right hand and vice versa if you hold it in your left hand), the leg is crocheted before you go on to the third part.
The third and last part of the work is the heel. The heel is crocheted last, after embroidering, because it is easier to make an embroidery pattern on the stocking when you can use the openings at both heel and top.

The basic pattern for the stocking is written out for a two-color stocking, with the toe, heel, and ribbing in color 1 and the foot and leg in color 2.

The colors are given as color 1 and color 2. You can decide which is color 1 or 2. Feel free to mix the sequence up for the individual stockings.

The striped stockings are crocheted from the same instructions, but, instead of shifting colors at the places given, just follow the suggestions for color changes in the section "Striped Christmas Stocking."

The stocking is crocheted in the round throughout.

If necessary, use a stitch marker to indicate the beginning and end of a round.

STRIPED CHRISTMAS STOCKING

The striped Christmas stocking is worked from the same instructions as for the toe-up stocking with the toe, heel, and cuff in a contrast color.

The color sequence is given below. Use the same color for the toe, heel, and cuff. The rest of the stocking is striped alternately on the 3rd and 4th rounds.

Color Sequence for the foot:
Rnds 1–4: Color 1.
Rnd 5: Color 2.
Rnd 6: Color 1.
Rnd 7: Color 2.
Rnd 8: Color 1.
Rnd 9: Color 2.
Rnd 10: Color 1.

Color Sequence for the leg:
Rnds 1–2: Color 1.
Rnd 3: Color 2.
Rnd 4: Color 1.
Rnd 5: Color 2.
Rnd 6: Color 1.
Rnd 7: Color 2.
Rnd 8: Color 1.
Rnd 9: Color 2.
Rnds 10–11: Color 1.

Ribbed cuff: Color 1.
Heel: Color 1.

FOOT

The first part of the Christmas stocking begins at the tip of the toe and continues to the foot. It is crocheted around in a spiral from the center of the toe and out.

Use a stitch marker to indicate the beginning and end of a round.

Begin with color 1 and hook U.S. D-3 (3 mm) (or hook size necessary to obtain given gauge).

Rnd 1: Work 8 sc around a magic ring = 8 sts.

Rnd 2: (Inc, 1 sc in next st) 4 times = 12 sts.

Rnd 3: (Inc, 1 sc in next st) 6 times = 18 sts.

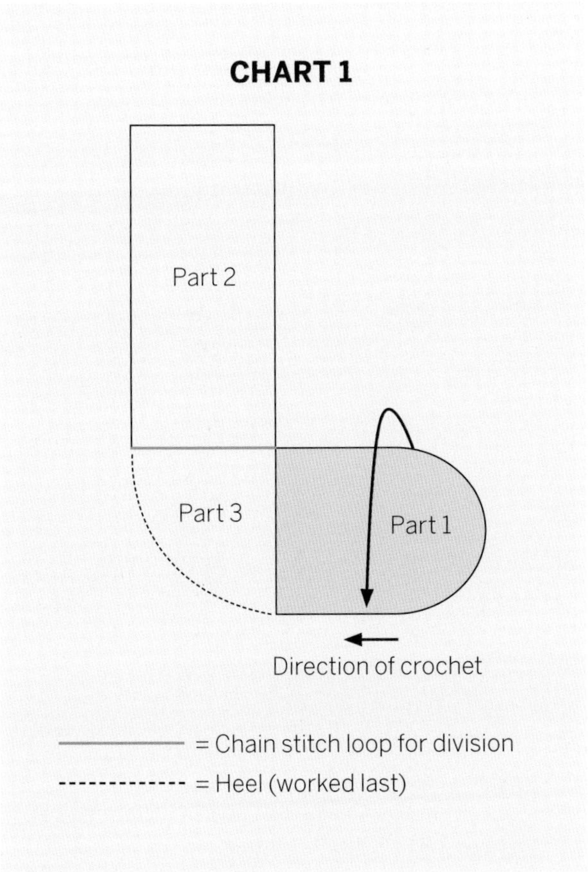

Rnd 4: 1 sc in each st around = 18 sts.

Change to color 2.
Rnds 5–10: 1 sc in each st around = 18 sts.

DIVIDING FOR HEEL AND LEG

On the next round, divide the piece into two parts by making a chain loop across the foot opening.

One side of the chain loop will be used to work part 2, the leg. The other side of the chain loop will be used to work part 3, the heel (see drawing at left).
Part 2 of the stocking continues as a direct extension of the final stitch on part 1.

After the division, you'll continue crocheting around in a spiral.
The chain for the division should be worked a bit loosely because it will draw in over the ankle if it is worked more tightly than the single crochet. You might go up a quarter or half hook size to make the chain loose enough.

The single crochet on the next round is worked into FL so the foot will point up and forward.

Rnd 1: Ch 10, skip the next 10 sts on 10th rnd of foot.
1 sc in FL of 11th st on foot Rnd 10.
1 sc in each of next 7 sts = 18 sts (10 ch + 8 sc).

On next rnd, work into loops on back of chain loop so the transition between heel and leg will be as invisible as possible. It might be a little hard to see where the first and last loops are placed because they are a little hidden under the chain loop. So, make sure you include all the stitches.

If it is too much of a challenge to crochet in the back loops of the chain, you can crochet through the chain as you normally would. This will create a different result, making a visible and a little more open transition between the leg and heel.

Rnd 2: 1 sc in each loop on back of the 10 ch, 1 sc in each of the next 8 sts = 18 sts.

Rnds 3–10: 1 sc in each st around = 18 sts. The last st on Rnd 10 is worked as a sl st to level the transition between the beginning and end of the rnd.

Cut yarn and weave in ends on WS of stocking.

On the next rnd, work ribbing the top of the stocking.

CHART 2

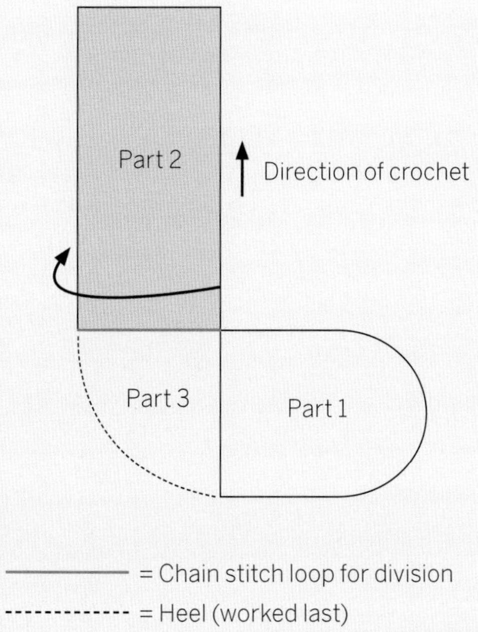

With color 2:
Rnd 11: Attach yarn with 1 sl st into st at center back of stocking. Ch 1 to heighten rnd, 1 dc in each st around = 18 sts.

Cut yarn and weave in ends.
The 2nd part of the stocking is now finished.

HEEL

The 3rd part of the stocking is the heel, which is crocheted around the opening between the foot and leg.
It begins on the foot, in the corner where the foot and leg meet.

Crochet first into the resting sc from Rnd 10 of foot. Then, crochet into the chain that divided the foot into two parts for leg and heel.

The heel is crocheted around in a spiral for the entire heel.

Use a stitch marker to indicate the beginning and end of each rnd.

Hold the stocking so the tip of the toe points in toward you and then heel points away from you while, at the same time, the leg points to the right.

The 1st sc is worked into the 1st sc on the foot.

The 1st st is an empty sc, not the sc where you already worked a sc, which lies in the corner between the foot and leg. This st belongs to Rnd 1 of the leg and is like an edging on the sides of the opening. If you crochet it here, there would be 2 sts too many on the rnd and the heel will be clumpy. If, when the crochet is finished, a little hole appears in this spot, you can sew it closed with a single stitch afterward.

With color 1:
Rnd 1: Attach yarn with 1 sl st into 1st sc of foot's resting sts. Work 1 sc in same st as sl st, 1 sc in each of next 9 sts on foot, 1 sc in each of next 10 sts of ch loop on leg = 20 sts.

Rnd 2: (Dec, 1 sc in each of next 6 sts, dec) 2 times = 16 sts.

Rnd 3: (Dec, 1 sc in each of next 4 sts, dec) 2 times = 12 sts.

Rnd 4: (Dec, 1 sc in each of next 2 sts, dec) 2 times = 8 sts.

Cut yarn, leaving an end long enough to sew remaining sts together.

Finish rnd by pulling opening together. Thread a needle with yarn end and insert needle in FL of st at center of opening and out. Do the same on every st around. After the last st, pull opening together by carefully tugging yarn end.

Cut yarn and weave in ends on WS of stocking.

CHART 3

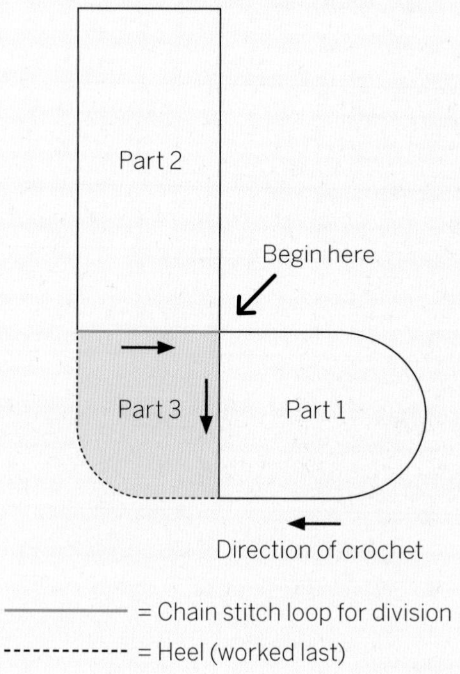

HANGING LOOP

If you plan on hanging the Christmas stockings, attach a loop at the top of the ribbing edge. A thin leather cord makes a nice finish for these wool stockings.

NUTCRACKER

The nutcracker has become an iconic symbol for the fairy-tale magic of Christmas. It comes in many styles and shapes. Most well-known are wooden figures with stern faces. Our version is crocheted with glitter yarn and is a little friendlier and smaller, so that it can stand on a windowsill or hang on the Christmas tree as a pretty ornament among the tree's other decorations.

Skill Level

The nutcracker is a project with a lot of geekiness required, for both crocheting and assembly. Therefore, it is only a project for you if you have had good experience with other projects, can decode the various stitch types and are competent with several different crochet techniques. The assembly requires some patience and it is not possible to skip this where the stakes are lowest. There are small pieces, each of which requires finesse for good results. The level of difficult drops significantly if you crochet the nutcracker with cotton yarn the first time around to get control over the techniques. In addition, a good work light is indispensable because the glitter yarn is difficult to work with if it is dark.

How to Achieve Good Results

Correct gauge is of the utmost importance for the finished results. The nutcracker's shape stands up with the help of decreases and increases, which are made as you work. Due to the yarn gauge, the nutcracker almost shapes itself when it is crocheted firmly and tightly at the given gauge. If you crochet loosely, the figure will be slack and it will be difficult to get the correct shape. If you crochet firmly and tightly and, at the same time, fill the nutcracker well, the assembly will be noticeably easier.

Technique Videos for the Nutcracker

These are the techniques: Chain stitch, slip stitch, single-crochet stitch, half-double crochet stitch, magic ring, crocheting around in a spiral, crocheting back and forth in rows, attaching yarn with a slip stitch, increasing, decreasing, joining 5 dc together (5-dc group), joining 8 dc together (8-dc group), crocheting in back loop, crocheting in the loop, crocheting on the back of a chain stitch, closing last round, attaching leg, attaching arm, hair for the nutcracker, shoulder decorations, assembly of nutcracker.

MATERIALS

Yarn and Fiberfill

Shiny Glimmergarn
7 g Red, Blue, or Green for jacket
6 g Red, Blue, or Green for pants and sleeve cuff

3 g White Gold for head and hands
3 g White Mother-of-Pearl for hair
10 g Black for boots, belt, hat, and mustache
3 g Gold for embellishment

6 g fiberfill

TOOLS

Recommended crochet hook: U.S. steel size 5 or 4 (1.75 or 2 mm)

Notions: Blunt tapestry needle to weave in ends, scissors

FINISHED MEASUREMENTS

Approx. 5¼" (13 cm) tall and 2" (5 cm) wide

Gauge

34 sts × 38 rnds single crochet worked around in a spiral with Shiny Glimmergarn from Krea Deluxe and hook U.S. steel size 4 (2 mm) = 4" × 4" / 10 × 10 cm. Adjust hook size to obtain correct gauge if necessary.

Gauge is of utmost importance for good results with this project.

The given gauge should be achieved with hook U.S. steel size 5 or 4 (1.75 or 2 mm). At the same time, you need to pull well on the yarn as you work. If you use hook U.S. steel size 5 (1.75 mm), you can get away with tightening the yarn a little less, which will make it more comfortable for your fingers to hold the Glimmergarn.

CONSTRUCTION

The nutcracker is crocheted from the bottom up in several steps.

Step 1: Boots and pants
Step 2: Arms/sleeves
Step 3 Upper body
Step 4: Head
Step 5: Belt and jacket decoration
Step 6: Hair
Step 7: Mustache, Beard, and Eyes
Step 8: Hat
Step 9: Assembly

Crochet Tips

Glimmergarn is not the easiest yarn to work with. The stitches are small and dark on the boots and Glimmergarn doesn't make it any easier. We recommend that you use a really good work light while you crochet. Natural daylight or a good work lamp, preferably with a magnifying glass, will help you on the way.

BOOTS

The soles of the boots are worked back and forth in rows for the first 7 rows. The 1st row is the back of the boot (heel) while the 7th row is the front toe tip. Each row is turned with ch 1 as a turning chain. When the sole is finished, continue around in a spiral around the sole.

BASE/SOLE

With Black and hook U.S. steel size 5 (1.75 mm) or hook needed for given gauge, ch 4—the last ch is a turning ch.

Row 1 is worked in the loops on back of the ch sts. When working into the loop, the first and last row of the piece will be joined. It will make it easier to crochet all the way around the sole of the boots later on.
Row 1: Beginning in 2nd ch from hook, work 1 sc in each loop on back of foundation ch = 3 sts.

Turn each row with ch 1 as a turning st.
Rows 2–6: 1 sc in each st across = 3 sts.

Row 7: 1 hdc in 1st st, 1 dc in next st, 1 hdc in last st = 3 sts.
The curve formed on Row 7 is the front tip/toe of the boot.

Cut yarn and weave in ends.

REST OF BOOT

The rest of the boot is crocheted around in a spiral. Rnd 1 begins at center back of the base/sole of the boot.
Use a stitch marker to indicate the beginning and end of the round.

Rnd 1: Attach yarn with 1 sl st in BL of center back st of the sole, 1 sc in same st as sl st. Work 1 sc in BL of next st, 5 sc along left side of sole, 1 sc each in BL of the 3 toe sts, 5 sc along right side of sole, 1 sc in BL of next st (last st of heel) = 16 sts.

Rnd 2: 1 sc in each st around = 16 sts.

Now begin shaping boot toe:
Rnd 3: 1 sc in each of next 6 sts.
Shape toe by joining the next 5 sts. Work these sts as dc and join as follows:
Yarn over hook (yok), insert hook into next st, yok, draw yarn through st, yok, draw yarn through 2 loops on hook. Rep *-* in next 4 sc = 6 loops on hook.
Yok, draw yarn through all loops on hook, 1 sc in each of next 5 sts = 12 sts.

Rnd 4: Dec, 1 sc in each st around = 11 sts.

Rnds 5–9: 1 sc in each st around = 11 sts.
Work last on Rnd 9 as a sl st to level transition between rounds.

Cut yarn and weave in ends on WS.

Fill lower part of boot.

Make a total of 2 boots the same way.

PANTS

The 1st rnd of a pant leg is worked through BL of sts in Rnd 9 of a boot to leave the FL free for crocheting on the gold edging later.
On Rnd 9 of the pant legs, they are crocheted together and then continue straight up until the color change for the jacket.

The pants are crocheted around in a spiral.

Use a stitch marker to indicate the beginning and end of the round.

Change to Green.
Rnd 1: Attach yarn with 1 sl st in BL of center back st of a boot, 1 sc in same st as sl st. Work 1 sc in BL of each st around = 11 sts.

Rnds 2–8: 1 sc in each st around = 11 sts.

Rnd 9: 1 sc in next st, inc, 1 sc in each of next 9 sts = 12 sts.
Work last on Rnd 9 as a sl st to level transition between rounds.

Cut yarn and weave in ends on WS.

Leave stitch marker in place.
Make a total of 2 legs the same way.

GOLD EDGING ON BOOTS

The gold edging on the boots is a simple round of slip stitches worked directly onto last rnd of the boot, into the FL left free when the pant leg was crocheted to the boot.

With Gold.
Turn boot so the opening of the pant leg is turned away from you and the foot faces you.
Attach yarn with 1 sl st in free FL of center back st of boot.
1 sl st in FL of same st as 1st sl st. Work 1 sl st in each st around and join rnd with 1 sl st = 11 sts.

Cut yarn and weave in ends on WS.

JOINING PANT LEGS

Rnd 10: Attach yarn with 1 sl st in 3rd st to left of stitch marker in leg no. 1. (Do not count st with marker. This is also shown on chart.)
The st where yarn was attached is now the beginning-of-rnd st. Place a new marker here for beginning and end of rnd.
Work 1 sc in same st as sl st, 1 sc in each of next 2 sts.

Now crochet in other leg.
With the legs held next to each other, use the st in leg 2 that is straight across from the last used st in leg no. 1 to join the legs together. This is the orange st on the chart.
If the legs don't point straight out when these sts are joined, the beginning of the rnd should be adjusted so they both point forward.

1 sc in each of next 11 sts on leg 2.
The last st of the 11 is the blue st on leg 2 on the chart below.
Now continue over the blue sts on leg 1 (the st directly after the last st that was crocheted on leg 1, before it was worked into leg 2), 1 sc in leg 1, 1 sc in each of next 8 sts = 24 sts.

Remove old markers on legs. The legs are now joined and the feet point forward.

CHART—PANT LEGS

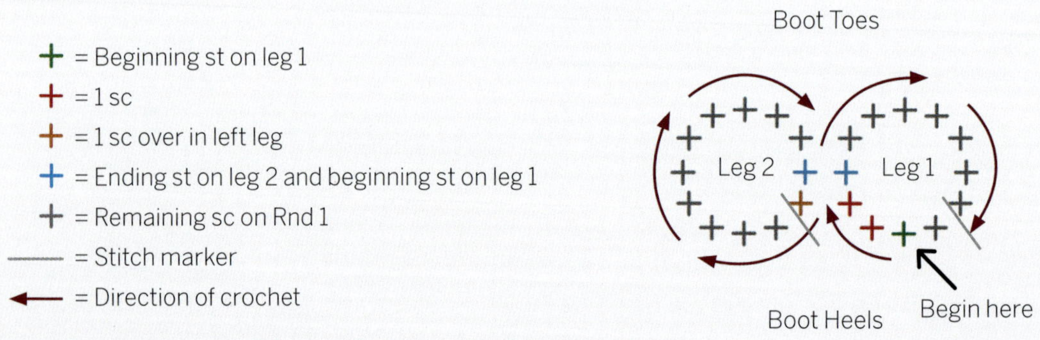

Fill boots and a little of each leg. Make sure you fill the boots well at heels and toes now because it will be difficult to do so later.

Rnds 11–14: 1 sc in each st around = 24 sts. The last st of Rnd 14 is a sl st to level transition between beginning and end of rnd.

Leave marker in place.

Cut yarn and weave in ends on WS.
The pants are now finished.

JACKET

Construction
The sleeves/arms will be joined to the body on Rnd 10 of the body. They should be crocheted before the body.

The sleeves/arms are worked from the bottom up. The first 2 rnds of the nutcracker's hands are worked in White Gold.

On Rnd 3, the color changes for the sleeve. Rnd 3 is worked in BL to leave the FL free for later crocheting the sleeve cuff.

Finally, the sleeve cuff is worked in the same color as for the pants. It is crocheted directly into the free front loops of sleeve Rnd 3.

Use a stitch marker to indicate the beginning and end of the round.

SLEEVES

With White Gold.
Rnd 1: Work 8 sc around a magic ring = 8 sts.

Rnd 2: 1 sc in each st around = 8 sts.

Change to Red.
On next rnd, work into BL so front loops are left free for working cuff into later.
Rnd 3: 1 sc in BL of each st around = 8 sts.

Rnds 4–13: 1 sc in each st around = 8 sts. The last st of Rnd 13 is a sl st to level transition between beginning and end of rnd.

Cut yarn and weave in ends on WS.

SLEEVE CUFF

With Green.
Rnd 1: Turn arm so hand points in toward you and arm points away from you.
Attach yarn with 1 sl st in one of the free FL on sleeve Rnd 3.
1 sc in same st as sl st, 1 sc in each st around = 8 sts.

Rnds 2–3: 1 sc in each st around = 8 sts. The last st of Rnd 3 is a sl st to level transition between beginning and end of rnd.

Cut yarn and weave in ends on WS.

Add a little filling to half of the sleeve to round it. Be careful not to fill so much that the sleeve widens or is pulled lengthwise.

Make a total of 2 sleeves/arms as described above.

UPPER BODY

Rnd 1 of the body is crocheted directly to Rnd 14 of the pants. Rnd 2 is worked into BL to leave FL free to use later for attaching the lower part of the jacket. The entire body is crocheted around in a spiral up to Rnd 10. The sleeves will be attached and joined with the body here.
Use a stitch marker to indicate the beginning and end of the round.

Continue with Red.
Rnd 1: Attach yarn with 1 sl st in center back st of pants—this corresponds to the 4th st to left of the stitch marker (the st with the marker does not count).
1 sc in same st as sl st—this st is new beginning of rnd. Place marker here and removed old marker. 1 sc in each st around = 24 sts.

On next rnd, work into BL and leave FL free for later crocheting of lower part of jacket.
Rnd 2: 1 sc in BL of each st around = 24 sts.

Rnd 3: 1 sc in each st around = 24 sts.

On next rnd, work an increase on each side of the body to give a V-shape to the upper body.
Rnd 4: 1 sc in each of next 7 sts, inc, 1 sc in each of next 11 sts, inc, 1 sc in each of next 4 sts = 26 sts.

Rnds 5–6: 1 sc in each st around = 26 sts.

On next rnd, increase again on each side of the body for the V-shape of upper body.
Rnd 7: 1 sc in each of next 8 sts, inc, 1 sc in each of next 12 sts, inc, 1 sc in each of next 4 sts = 28 sts.

Rnds 8–9: 1 sc in each st around = 28 sts.

JOINING SLEEVES AND BODY

The sleeves are joined to the body on the next rnd. Use the same technique as for joining the pant legs.
Rnd 10: 1 sc in each of next 9 sts on back.
1 sc over on sleeve 1.
1 sc in each of next 7 sts of sleeve.
1 sc over on body (in st directly at side of st last made on body).

1 sc in each of next 13 sts on chest.
1 st over on sleeve 2.
1 sc in each of next 7 sts on sleeve.
1 sc over on body (in st directly at side of st last made on body).

1 sc in each of next 4 sts on back = 44 sts.

Rnds 11–12: 1 sc in each st around = 44 sts.

Rnd 13: 1 sc in each of next 8 sts, dec, 1 sc in each of next 6 sts, dec, 1 sc in each of next 12 sts, dec, 1 sc in each of next 6 sts, dec, 1 sc in each of next 4 sts = 40 sts.

Fill legs, body, and sleeves.

The nutcracker's shape will be correct when you fill out all the curves, forms, and body parts. However, it will only be the right shape if you fill it carefully. The body should be very firm so it can't be pressed out of shape. If there is too little filling, the nutcracker won't look right and it will be difficult to assemble correctly.
Add a little filling at a time, gradually adding more and more to the boots and up through the legs and body.
At the same time, it is important to be careful when filling so the fiberfill doesn't clump into little balls or widen the sts so holes appear in the piece.

Shape the shoulders on the next rnd.
Rnd 14: 1 sc in each next 8 sts.
Shape the shoulders by crocheting the next 8 sts together. The sts are dc joined at the top as follows:

Yarn over hook (yok), insert hook into next st, yok, draw yarn through st, yok, draw yarn through 2 loops on hook. Rep *-* in next 7 sc = 9 loops on hook.
Yok and draw yarn through all loops on hook, 1 sc in each of next 12 sts, join 8 sts as above for first shoulder, 1 sc in each of next 4 sts = 26 sts.

On the next 2 rnds, crochet the jacket neck.
Rnd 15: (1 sc in next st, dec, 1 sc in each of next 3 sts, dec) 2 times, (1 sc in each of next 2 sts, dec) 2 times, 1 sc in each of next 2 sts = 20 sts.

Rnd 16: 1 sc in each st around = 20 sts.
The last st of Rnd 16 is a sl st to level transition between beginning and end of rnd.

Cut yarn and weave in ends on WS.
Fill rest of body.

LOWER PART OF JACKET

Crochet the lower part of the jacket into the free stitch loops on Rnd 2 of the upper body. This part will sit outside the pants. The jacket is open at center front on the nutcracker. It is worked back and forth in rows beginning at center front, around the back, and then opposite side of front. The center front st is not used so this will be a place for the gold edging on the two flaps.
Turn each row with ch 1 as a turning st.

Turn the body so the neck opening turns in toward you, the legs point away from you, and the front of the nutcracker faces up.
Row 1: Find the center st on the front of the nutcracker. Attach yarn with 1 sl st in the st to the left of the center st (if you crochet from right to left), 1 sc in same st as sl st, 1 sc in each of next 10 sts, inc, 1 sc in each of next 11 sts = 24 sts.

Turn work and crochet back:
Rows 2–6: 1 sc in each st across = 24 sts.

To create a sharp finish, work the next row as sl sts in FL.
Row 7: 1 sl st in FL of each st across = 24 sts.

Cut yarn and weave in ends on WS.

Work a row of sc on each side of the jacket opening to finish it with a gold edging.

RIGHT FRONT EDGING OF JACKET

Turn body so the right side faces down and you can crochet from the lower tip of the jacket leftward along the edge.

Attach yarn with 1 sl st in the st at very bottom tip of jacket.
1 sc in same st as sl st; evenly space 5 sc along the rest of the edging up to the top of the flap = 6 sts.

Cut yarn and weave in ends on WS.

LEFT FRONT EDGING OF JACKET

Turn body so the right side faces down and you can crochet from the top of the flap down to the lower tip of the jacket.

Attach yarn with 1 sl st in the st at very top of flap.

1 sc in same st as sl st; evenly space 5 sc along the rest of the edging up to the tip of the flap = 6 sts.

Cut yarn, leaving an end long enough to sew the 3 top sts together to close the jacket a little.
weave in ends on WS.

HEAD

The nutcracker's head is an egg-shaped, oblong ball. The shape makes it easy for the hat to sit neatly and stably on the head. It is worked around in a spiral from the bottom up for the whole head.

Use a stitch marker to indicate the beginning and end of the round.

With White Gold.
Rnd 1: Work 6 sc around a magic ring = 6 sts.

Rnd 2: (inc) 6 times = 12 sts.

Rnd 3: (inc, 1 sc in next st) 6 times = 18 sts.

Rnd 4: (inc, 1 sc in each of next 2 sts) 6 times = 24 sts.

Rnd 5: (1 sc in each of next 3 sts, inc) 6 times = 30 sts.

Rnds 6–7: 1 sc in each st around = 30 sts.

Rnd 8: (1 sc in each of next 8 sts, dec) 3 times = 27 sts.

Rnd 9: 1 sc in each st around = 27 sts.

Rnd 10: (1 sc in each of next 7 sts, dec) 3 times = 24 sts.

Rnds 11–13: 1 sc in each st around = 24 sts.

Rnd 14: (Dec, 1 sc in each of next 2 sts) 6 times = 18 sts.

Rnd 15: (Dec, 1 sc in next st) 6 times = 12 sts.

Fill head so it is firm and tight.

Rnd 16: (Dec) 6 times = 6 sts.

Tighten the round by pulling the opening together as follows: Cut yarn, leaving an end long enough to use for sewing the opening together. Thread a needle with the yarn end and insert the needle into st FL from the center of the hole and outward. Do the same with every st around.
After the last st is caught, pull the hole together by carefully tugging on the yarn end.
Weave in end on WS.

Press the head so it is egg-shaped and has a flat base.

Sew the head firmly to the body between Rnds 3–4 of the head as counted from the bottom up.

BELT

The belt consists of a single row of sc. By crocheting into the loop on back of a ch row, the belt will have a uniform look on the top and bottom of the sts.

When the 1st row is worked in the loops on back of the chain, the chain should be a bit loose because it will draw in when you crochet into it. If necessary, use a hook one quarter or one half larger for the foundation chain.

With Black, ch 26—the last st is a turning ch.

Row 1: Go to back of foundation chain and work 1 sc in 2nd ch from hook, 1 sc in each loop across = 25 sts.

Cut yarn, leaving an end long enough to use for sewing the belt around the waist.

ATTACHING THE BELT

Place the belt at the waist just over the jacket flaps. The belt should be 1 st smaller than the circumference of the nutcracker's waist.

Tighten the belt so the ends meet at the center back of the nutcracker.
Sew the ends together and make a couple of stitches along the top of the sts so the belt doesn't bulge out.

At the center front of the belt, with Gold, make a couple of stitches for a buckle. Sew them vertically over the belt and make a horizontal stitch at the top and bottom between the two vertical stitches.

Weave in ends on WS.

CHEST DECORATION

The nutcracker's chest is decorated with Gold embellishments. The rounded curve is a chain strip of 25 ch sts. The ends should be 9¾"–11¾" (25–30 cm) longer and can be used to sew the chain to the nutcracker and, at the same time, make horizontal stripes on his chest.

With Gold, ch 25 sts.

Pin each end of the foundation chain to the shoulders.

The bottom tip of the curve is placed 2 rows above the belt buckle.

Use the yarn end from the chain to sew on the chain by weaving sts up and down from ch st to ch st.

Now sew the stripes across the chest.

Use a ch st on one side as a starting point and a ch directly across as the end point.

Make four stripes horizontally across the chest with 2 rows between each.

Cut yarn and weave in ends on WS.

SHOULDER DECORATIONS

The nutcracker has impressive shoulder decorations, called epaulettes, crocheted with gold yarn. Double crochet sts are worked around a magic ring to create a half circle. Then rows of single crochet go down the shoulders. Finally, the epaulettes are attached to the nutcracker.

With Gold.
Row 1: Work 8 dc around a magic ring.
Tighten the magic ring so the dc form a half circle. To stabilize the decoration, work sc over the surface of the half circle's flat part around the dc posts and into the magic ring hole.
Work 2 sc around the post of the 1st dc 1 sc in hole of magic ring, 2 sc on post of 2nd dc.

The top part of the shoulder decoration Is now finished and you'll continue with sc down around the shoulders, working back and forth in rows.
Row 2: Ch 1 to add height to the row, 1 sc around post of last sc of Row 1, 1 sc in BL of each of the 8 dc, 1 sc around post of 1st sc on flat piece of half circle = 10 sts.

Turn work with ch 1 as turning ch.
Row 3: 1 sc in each st across = 10 sts.

Cut yarn, leaving an end long enough sew the shoulder decoration securely onto the nutcracker.

Make 2 epaulettes total.

ATTACHING THE SHOULDER DECORATIONS

Pin the epaulettes into place on the shoulders. Thread a needle with the yarn end and sew the piece securely along the flat part of the half circle and down the shoulder of the nutcracker with a couple of stitches.

Now sew the corners down so the entire epaulette lies on top of the sleeve and down the shoulder without stretching.

JACKET COLLAR

To finish the upper body, make a chain as a jacket collar.

With Gold, ch 23 sts.
Lay the chain around the neck where the jacket and head are joined.

The chain row ends should meet precisely without stretching or the ch will be loose and slide around. It is better to chain fewer or more sts at the end than to stretch the chain too much and make a slack collar.

Sew the ends of the chain cord at center back of the body where the head and jacket meet.

Then sew the ends of the chain together and weave in last end inside nutcracker.

HAIR

The hair is made with simple ch st and sc worked back and forth in rows.

On one end, make a chain and then work sc along it on the next row. This allows the chain to form small curled tufts.

On the 1st row, work the first 3 sc though the ch sts, but, the last 5 sc are worked into the loops on back of the foundation chain. The top and bottom of the 5 sc will become united, which affects the look when you sew the hair on.

Row 1 and all odd-numbered rows are the RS. This is also the way the tufts curl.

Turn each row with ch 1 as a turning ch.

With White Mother-of-Pearl, ch 9 sts—the last st is a turning ch.

Row 1: Beginning in 2nd ch from hook, work 1 sc in each of next 3 ch, 1 sc in loops of next 5 sts on back of in each foundation ch = 8 sts.

Row 2: 1 sc in each of next 5 sts, ch 4—5 sc and 4 ch.

Row 3: 1 sc in 2nd ch from hook, 1 sc in each of next 2 ch, 1 sc in each of next 5 sts on row = 8 sts.

Repeat Rows 2–3 a total of 11 times for a total of 12 curled tufts.

The curls are the bottom of the hair while the opposite side is the top of the hair. The first and last rows are, therefore, the sides of the hair, which are placed at the front next to the face.

To finish the hair, make a row of sc on top of the hair as follows:
Ch 1 to heighten the row.
Turn work so you can crochet over the long side without curls (the top of the hair).
Work 20–22 sc evenly spaced over the top of the hair.

Cut yarn, leaving one end long enough to sew the hair securely to the head.

Weave in all ends on WS.

ATTACHING THE HAIR

The top of the hair is placed in the ridge between Rnds 6 and 7 of the head as counted from the top down. The curls should lie a bit above the shoulder decorations.
Pin the hair firmly in place to hold it while you attach it.

Sew along the top of the hair as follows:
Step 1: Insert needle behind a stitch leg in the ridge between Rnds 6 and 7 of the head.
Step 2: Bring needle through.
Step 3: Insert needle in from the back of FL of hair.
Step 4: Go back into same st on head where the yarn came out.

Repeat Steps 1–4 all across top of hair.

Now use small stitches to sew up and down along the edge of the hair at the face on both sides.

Finally, make a couple of stitches at the base of the hair a little over the curls so the hair lies in toward the head and neck.

Weave in ends on WS.

MUSTACHE

The mustache consists of two small drop-shaped pieces, one for each part of the mustache. They are each crocheted separately and attached afterward.

All the sts are worked into the loops on back of the foundation chain.

With Black, ch 5 sts—the last 2 sts are turning ch sts.

On the back of the chain, work 1 hdc in 3rd ch from hook, 1 sl st into each of next 2 ch = 3 sts.

Cut yarn and make a tight knot on the two ends for a little tip in at the sl st. Weave in one end on back of mustache. The other end will be used to sew on the mustache.

Make a total of 2 mustache pieces.

ATTACHING THE MUSTACHE

Place the mustache on the head over the 12th rnd as counted from the top down, and, at the same time, with 1 st between each piece.

Sew the two pieces firmly to the head by making a couple of stitches at the top and bottom of the hdc and along the edges. A thin, sharp curved needle is a big help here.

Weave in ends securely.

WHITE BEARD

The white beard consists of seven strands of yarn the same color as the hair. The yarn is twisted around the stitches on the round of the head right below the mustache.
The beard is then trimmed into shape.

With White Mother-of-Pearl, cut seven strands 8" (20 cm) long.

Fold the strands in the middle.

Thread a needle with two of the folded ends.

Insert needle behind the round directly under the mustache. Make sure only the ends come through, and not the fold.
Pull the two ends through the fold and tighten so the yarn is firmly against the round on the head.

Do likewise with all the strands. Place two strands in the same place so they'll lie tightly together and above each other. If necessary, use more than seven ends for a fuller beard.

Trim the yarn ends for a pointed beard so the longest part of the point ends at the fourth braid on the chest and the shortest reaches down to the third braid as counted from the top down.

EYES

With Black.
Each eye is made with a single stitch sewn above the 9th row as counted from the top down. Place the eyes with 4 stitch holes/5 sts between each.

Weave in ends securely on WS.

HAT

The hat is oblong-shaped with a brim at the front, a little gold braid, and a little gold ball decorating the hat's crown (the crown is the part of the hat that sits on the head).

The hat is crocheted from the top down, around in a spiral. After the 15th rnd, the working yarn is put aside while you make the brim. The brim is a simple row of single crochet, worked with a separate strand at the center of the round. After that, you'll take up the yarn from Rnd 15 and continue, crocheting an edging all around the crown as well as across the brim.

Finally, the gold braid and gold ball are crocheted and sewn onto the hat before the hat is attached.

Use a stitch marker to indicate the beginning and end of the rounds.

With Black, cut a strand about 39½" (1 meter) long and set it to the side. It will be used for the brim after Rnd 15. Continue to the hat below.

Rnd 1: Work 6 sc around a magic ring = 6 sts.

Rnd 2: (Inc) 6 times = 12 sts.

Rnd 3: (Inc, 1 sc in next st) 6 times = 18 sts.

Rnd 4: (1 sc in each of next 2 sts, inc) 6 times = 24 sts.

Rnd 5: 1 sc in next st (inc, 1 sc in each of next 3 sts) 5 times, inc, 1 sc in each of next 2 sts = 30 sts.

On the next rnd, work only into BL so the hat crown can be folded down sharply.

Rnd 6: 1 sc in BL of each st around = 30 sts.

Rnd 7: 1 sc in each st around = 30 sts.

Rnd 8: 1 sc in each of next 5 sts, dec, 1 sc in each of next 23 sts = 29 sts.

Rnd 9: 1 sc in each st around = 29 sts.

Rnd 10: 1 sc in each of next 16 sts, dec, 1 sc in each of next 11 sts = 28 sts.

Rnd 11: 1 sc in each st around = 28 sts.

Rnd 12: 1 sc in each of next 13 sts, dec, 1 sc in each of next 13 sts = 27 sts.

Rnd 13: 1 sc in each st around = 27 sts.

Rnd 14: 1 sc in each of next 13 sts, inc, 1 sc in each of next 13 sts = 28 sts.

Rnd 15: 1 sc in each st around = 28 sts.

Set working yarn aside and continue to hat brim

BRIM

Hold hat so the opening for the head points away from you and the top of the hat points in toward you.

Use the saved 39½" (1 meter) long strand to crochet the brim.

The row is crocheted in front loops only so the brim will point slightly forward.
Row 1: Attach yarn with 1 sl st in a FL of the 10th st to the left of the rnd marker. Do not count the marked st.
Work 1 sc in same st as sl st, 1 sc in next in FL of each of next 5 sts = 6 sts.

Cut yarn and weave in end down along side of brim and on WS of hat crown.

EDGING OF CROWN AND BRIM

Pick up yarn left on Rnd 15 and continue to last rnd as follows:
(Make sure you crochet the slip sts a bit loosely so they don't tighten and draw the crown in.)

1 sl st in FL of each st up to brim.
1 sc at edge of brim,
on front of brim, crochet 1 sc in each st,
1 sc at edge of brim,
1 sl st in FL of each st to end of rnd.

Cut yarn and weave in ends.

Decorations on Hat

The hat is decorated with a little gold braid and a gold ball on top.

Gold Braid

For the gold braid, crochet a chain 2" (5 cm) long. The ends of the chain and the last st are used to sew the braid on at each side of the hat.

Thread needle with one end and insert it into the hat between Rnds 3 and 4 as counted from the top down. The placement should correspond to the center of the shoulder when the hat is on and the brim points straight ahead.
Weave in end firmly on WS of hat.
Do the same on the other side of the braid and hat.

Gold Ball

Work 6 sc around a magic ring and then draw sts together into a ball as follows:

Cut yarn, leaving one end long enough to sew ball onto hat. Thread needle with yarn end and beginning at center of ring, insert needle into FL of st and then out; repeat on each of the sts. After the last st is caught, pull the sts together into a ball, carefully tugging on the yarn end.
If necessary sew around the sts once more for a completely round ball.

Now sew the ball firmly to the top of the hat.
Weave in ends securely on WS.

ATTACHING THE HAT

Using a thin, curved needle will make this step much easier. You can also make the assembly easier while you sew if you hold the nutcracker so the feet point away from you and the hat points in toward you.

Add filling in the top of the hat. If you want a very flat top on the hat, you can cut out a cardstock circle the same diameter as the hat. Glue the paper into the hat before you add filling.

Pin the hat onto the head so it is over the hair and the brim points forward.

Work as follows:
Thread a thin needle with the same yarn as for the hat. Knot one end.

Insert the needle into the hat from the WS and out in a st straight over the sl st right above the hairline on the head.
Bring yarn through, making sure the knot stays securely inside the hat on WS.

Sew the hat securely to the head as follows:
Step 1: Insert needle behind the sl st on hat and out at base of st.
Step 2: Bring yarn through again.
Step 3: Go behind one of the sc at top of hairline.
Step 4: Bring yarn through again.
Step 5: Insert needle behind next sl st on hat from below and out at top of st.

Repeat Steps 1–5 all around the hairline.

The stitches should lie smoothly along the hat without pulling the hat in.
Sew around several times to make sure that the hat sits evenly and uniformly on the head.

Weave in ends securely, before trimming yarn.

FINAL ASSEMBLY

CROSSED LACES ON THE BOOTS

To finish the boots, embroider small crosses as laces on the front of each boot leg.
The top crosses are sewn into the holes above and below the 2nd-to-last rnd. There will be an empty stitch hole between the corners of the crosses.
The crosses at the bottom are the same size as the top crosses and placed as an extension of the base of the top cross.

SEAMING THE LEGS

So the legs and boots will sit tightly, sew them with the same color yarn they were crocheted in.
It will be helpful to use a long needle, such a s a doll needle so you can sew through both legs at a time.
Stitch from the outer side of one leg, through both legs, and out on the outer side of the other leg.
Go one stitch hole down and sew the same way, but, in the opposite direction.
Tighten yarn slightly, but do it carefully so you don't pull the stitches together and make small notches and bulges in the legs.
Continue the same way so the legs are sewn together at both top and bottom.
Weave in ends securely on WS.

SEAMING THE BOOTS

Sew the boots together as for the legs using the same color as for the boots. If the boots bulge at the top, you can make a couple of stitches up through the top and down through the bottom so the top of the toe will flatten out more.

Weave in all ends securely on WS.

SEAMING THE BODY

The body is sewn together as for the legs, from side to side through both arms, at the sleeve cuff as well as at the shoulders to pull them all together slightly.
Use the same color as the body and sleeve cuffs to sew with.

Weave in all ends securely on WS.

GIFT BAGS

Many children and other Christmas-loving souls enjoy opening Advent calendars in December. These crocheted gift bags are nice to hang in calendar formation, packed with surprises to be opened each day of Advent. They'll be anticipated every year when Christmas nears. A little gift marker with a number can embellish the bags while they hang. The bags can also be used for packaging Christmas gifts for those you hold dear and it's brilliant that they can be used year after year.

Skill Level

Gift bags are a project most can work on even if they require some practice at holding the yarn and crocheting evenly with the jacquard crochet technique. Don't give up on the first part of the piece where the colors change, even if it is a bit difficult to crochet. It will be easier as soon as your hands memorize the moves. The level of difficulty becomes markedly lower if the figures are embroidered on the bags with cross stitch later. Much of the work is repetitive, using only the most general techniques and basic stitches. If you have not had any previous experience with color changes, it's a good idea to begin with a simple pattern such as the Christmas goat and embroider the red bands afterward.

How to Achieve Good Results

If the figures are embroidered on the bags, gauge is important for the finished results. If the bags are crocheted more loosely than at the given gauge, the cross stitch will be open and will not cover the background.

If you crochet the figures on the bag, the gauge is not as important. Instead, you should be careful to crochet evenly and not too tightly when changing colors. It is recommended that you block the bags before seaming them so the sides won't fold in and skew the bag shaping.

Technique Videos for Gift Bags

These are the techniques: Chain stitch, slip stitch, single-crochet stitch, crocheting back and forth in rows, crocheting around in a spiral, attaching yarn with a slip stitch, increasing, crocheting in the loop on the back of a chain stitch, crocheting around a chain loop, jacquard crochet, changing colors, crocheting the first and second rounds of the base, embroidered cross stitch, crocheted I-cord, assembling gift bags.

MATERIALS

Yarn

Organic Cotton

90 g color 46, Sand for one bag and cord (without figures)

For all the figures, you'll need:
10 g color 01, Natural White
10 g color 09, Mustard
5 g color 26, Dark Blue
15 g color 30, Brown
15 g color 35, Red
10 g color 42, Moss Green
5 g color 45, Bottle Green
10 g color 52, Cognac

TOOLS

Recommended crochet hook: U.S. size C-2 (2.5 mm)

Notions: Blunt embroidery needle to seaming and embroidery, scissors

FINISHED MEASUREMENTS

Approx. 10¾" (27 cm) long and 6½" (16.5 cm) wide when bag lays flat

---

Gauge

32 sts × 37 rows crocheted back and forth in rows with Organic Cotton and hook U.S. size C-2 (2.5 mm) = 4" × 4" / 10 × 10 cm.

Adjust hook size to obtain correct gauge if necessary.

CONSTRUCTION

The gift bags each have several parts.

The first part is the bottom of the bag, crocheted in rounds. The base is shaped as a rectangle with rounded corners.

The sides are crocheted next, back and forth in rows. Each side is worked separately. Before the sides are seamed together, they are edged with single-crochet.

Finally, the top is crocheted with a casing running around both sides.

The base, top, and sides are all crocheted with Sand. The motifs are worked on one side and the bags are then finished a cord through the casing.

BASE OF THE BAG

The bottom of each bag is crocheted around a foundation chain consisting of a chain and a row of single crochet in the loops on the back of the chain stitches. By working single crochet in the backs of the loops on back of the foundation chain, it is possible to crochet at the top and bottom of the foundation chain as well as at the sides of the chain. Using this method means that you can then crochet around in a spiral for the following rounds. When crocheting the 1st row in the loops on the back of the chain stitches, the chains should be a bit loose because the chain will pull in when you crochet into the loops. If necessary, use a hook a quarter or half size larger for the foundation chain.

You will increase (inc) on the first 6 rnds and then continue straight up through Rnd 11.

With Sand and hook U.S. C-2 (2.5 mm) or hook necessary for correct gauge, ch 41—the last st is a turning ch.

Beginning in 2nd ch from hook, work 1 sc in each loop on back of chain = 40 sts.

Place a stitch marker in the last st of the row. This will be a big help because, otherwise, it is not easy to find the end of the 1st rnd.

On the first rnd, you'll increase to form corners at each end and on each side of the foundation chain.

Rnd 1:
Turn work so you can crochet in the base of the sts of the foundation chain.

Ch 2 (side 1)—this 1st ch adds height to the rnd. The 2nd ch is a turning ch on the other end of the row. By crocheting the last ch, it is possible to crochet on the side/end of the foundation chain. Only the 1st ch is included in the total stitch count; the 2nd ch is a turning ch.

Inc in the next st (corner 1).
1 sc in each of next 38 sts (side 2).
Inc in last st (corner 2).

Ch 1 to round the end of the row so you can crochet in the top of the sts on foundation chain (side 3).

Skip turning ch on side of foundation chain; turn work so you can crochet under both st loops on top of the sts on foundation chain.

Inc in next st (corner 3),.
1 sc in each of next 38 sts (side 4).

Inc in last st (corner 4),
= 86 sts (84 sc + 2 ch —the ch at each end counts as sides 1 and 3).

Now you can continue, working around in a spiral for the rest of the base. On the next 4 rnds, you'll increase 4 sts on each rnd.

It is important that the corners be symmetrical and aligned over each other to create a rectangle. If you realize that the corners are staggered, you need to move the placement of the increases.

Use a stitch marker to indicate the beginning/end of the round.

Rnd 2:
1 sc in end st of foundation chain,
1 sc in next st (side 1),
Inc (corner 1),
1 sc in each of next 38 sts (side 2).
Inc (corner 2),
1 sc in next st),
1 sc in end st of previous rnd,
1 sc in next st (side 3),
Inc (corner 3),
1 sc in each of next 38 sts (side 4).
Inc (corner 4),
1 sc in next st (belongs to side 1)
= 90 sts.

Rnd 3:
1 sc in each of next 3 sts, inc, 1 sc in each of next 38 sts, inc.
1 sc in each of next 5 sts, inc, 1 sc in each of next 38 sts, inc.
1 sc in each of next 2 sts = 94 sts.

Rnd 4:
1 sc in each of next 4 sts, inc, 1 sc in each of next 39 sts, inc.
1 sc in each of next 6 sts, inc, 1 sc in each of next 39 sts, inc.
1 sc in each of next 2 sts = 98 sts.

Rnd 5:
1 sc in each of next 4 sts, inc, 1 sc in each of next 41 sts, inc.
1 sc in each of next 6 sts, inc, 1 sc in each of next 41 sts, inc.
1 sc in each of next 2 sts = 102 sts.

On the next rnd, there only two increases, placed at each end of the rnd.

Rnd 6: 1 sc in next st, inc, 1 sc in each of next 50 sts, inc, 1 sc in each of next 49 sts = 104 sts.

Rnds 7–11: 1 sc in each st around = 104 sts.
The last st on Rnd 11 is a sl st to level the transition between beginning and end of rnd.

The base of the bag is now finished. Leave stitch marker in. Cut yarn and weave in ends.

SIDES OF THE BAG

The sides are the next part of this project. They are each crocheted separately, back and forth in rows. Each side has 51 sts. The center st on the short sides of the base is not used. This st will "rest" until the sides are seamed later on.

The first side is worked in a single color (the same color as the base). The pattern motif is worked on the other side of the gift bag. The pattern can either be crocheted in as you make the side or embroidered on later.

FIRST SIDE OF BAG

The sides of the bag begin on the RS of the bag.
Row 1: Attach yarn with 1 sl st in 3rd st to left of stitch marker—this st is not included in stitch counts.
Work 1 sc in same st as sl st and then 1 sc in each of next 50 sts = 51 sts.

Turn each row with ch 1 as a turning ch.
Rows 2–77: 1 sc in each st across = 51 sts.
Cut yarn and weave in ends on WS.

SECOND SIDE OF BAG

Attach yarn with 1 sl st in 2nd st to left of last stitch on first side, so 1 resting st remains on the base between the two sides of the bag.

Note: Row 1 has the same stitch structure as for the sts worked in the round. That is to say, that Row 1 is the same as Rnds 1–11 on the base. Don't forget to count it into the total number of rows because it is important for the look of the patterns, when they are crocheted or embroidered so they begin on the correct row.

If Embroidering the Figures

If you are going to embroider the figures on the bag, work the second side as for the first side of the gift bag. When the side is finished, embroider the figure in cross stitch using the chart for your chosen pattern. See all the charts on pages 188–193.

1 square on the chart = 1 cross stitch embroidered with the color shown on the chart.

Cross stitch is worked over four holes on the crocheted surface. The four holes correspond to the holes around 1 crocheted st.
Weave in all ends on WS of work.

If Crocheting the Figures

If you are going to crochet the figures with jacquard crochet, work them as explained for gift bag, side 1, while, at the same time, beginning the color changes on Row 6.
When the first 5 rows are finished, continue from the chart for the figure you have chosen.

Don't forget to count Row 1 as explained above.

The charts feature arrows on both right and left sides of the chart.
These arrows show the direction for reading the chart and the direction of crochet.
At the same time, they also indicate which side of the work you are crocheting on (RS or WS).

Row 1 and all odd-numbered rows are crocheted on the RS. The arrow here points to the left.
All rows with an arrow that point to the left are worked on the RS.

The next row, row 2 of the pattern, is worked on WS. The arrow here points to the right.
All rows with an arrow that point to the right are worked on the WS.

1 square on chart = 1 sc st crocheted with the color shown on the chart.

Weave in all ends on WS of work.

SINGLE-CROCHET EDGING

To stabilize the bag sides, work a single-crochet edging along the long sides of the bag. In addition, the edging makes it easier to seam the sides evenly and uniformly.

The single-crochet edging with RS facing on each of the long sides. The edging on the right side is worked from the base up and, on the left side, from the top down.

The number of sts to crochet depends on how the sts are spaced and how tightly. As a starting point, work 1 sc for each row, skipping every 5th row.

The edging should neither bulge nor draw in. If the edging bulges, there are too many sts. If it draws in, there are too few sts.
At the same time, it is important that you have the same number of sts on each side (or as much as possible) so you can seam the bag evenly.

Work as follows:
Attach yarn with 1 sl st at top or base on one of the bag's sides.
Work 1 sc in same st as sl st. Continue with sc all along the side.

When you've finished sc along one edge, cut yarn and weave in ends on WS.

SEAMING

Lay the two sides flat with edge against edge and RS up. Make sure that the rows on the sides align.

Pin the sides in a couple of spots to hold them in place while you sew. This is especially important if there are not exactly the same number of sts on each edge.

Use overcast st to seam the sides on RS of work. Sew through FL on the side turned toward you and in BL on the side turned away from you. Insert needle in from the same side with every st.

Cut yarn.

CASING AT TOP OF GIFT BAG

The top of the bag is crocheted around in a spiral in single crochet with the same color as for the bag. You'll make holes for the drawstring on Rnd 3.

Use a stitch marker to indicate the beginning and end of each rnd.

Rnd 1: Attach yarn with 1 sl st in seam, 1 sc in same st as sl st, 1 sc in each st around and, at the same time, 1 sc in seam on opposite side of bag = 104 sts.

Rnd 2: 1 sc in each st around = 104 sts.

On next rnd, make holes on casing for drawstring.

Rnd 3: (1 sc in each of next 2 sts, ch 1, skip 1 st) 34 times, 1 sc in each of next 2 sts = 104 sts.
The first and last holes of the casing are spaced further apart than the other holes because the ends of the drawstring will go through them.

Rnd 4: 1 sc in each st and 1 sc round each ch loop around = 104 sts.

Rnds 5–11: 1 sc in each st around = 104 sts.
The last st on Rnd 11 is a sl st to level the transition between beginning and end of rnd.

The top of the bag is now finished.

Cut yarn and weave in ends on WS.

CROCHETED I-CORD

The cord for the casing is a crocheted I-cord. It functions as for a crochet chain but has an extra yarn around hook for each st worked. The technique is easy and the cord can be crocheted relatively quickly once you learn the technique.

Work as follows:
Make a skip knot as for beginning a ch st. The yarn end should be about 2¼ yd (2 m) long so you can crochet with both that end and the end from the yarn ball.

Hold the yarn, with both ends held firmly. The yarn from the yarn ball is placed backmost and the long end foremost.

1. Yarn around hook with front strand—the hook should come from behind the yarn.
2. Yarn around hook with back strand—the hook should come from front of the yarn.
3. Bring yarn through yarnover and loop on hook.

Repeat steps 1–3 until cord is 21¾"–23¾" (55–60 cm) long.

Cut yarn.

Thread ends on a large blunt tapestry needle and draw cord through holes on casing.

Weave in ends into cord.

Knot ends of drawstring cord so it won't come out of casing when you use bag.

Charts

GIFT BAGS

CHART 1—CANDY CANE

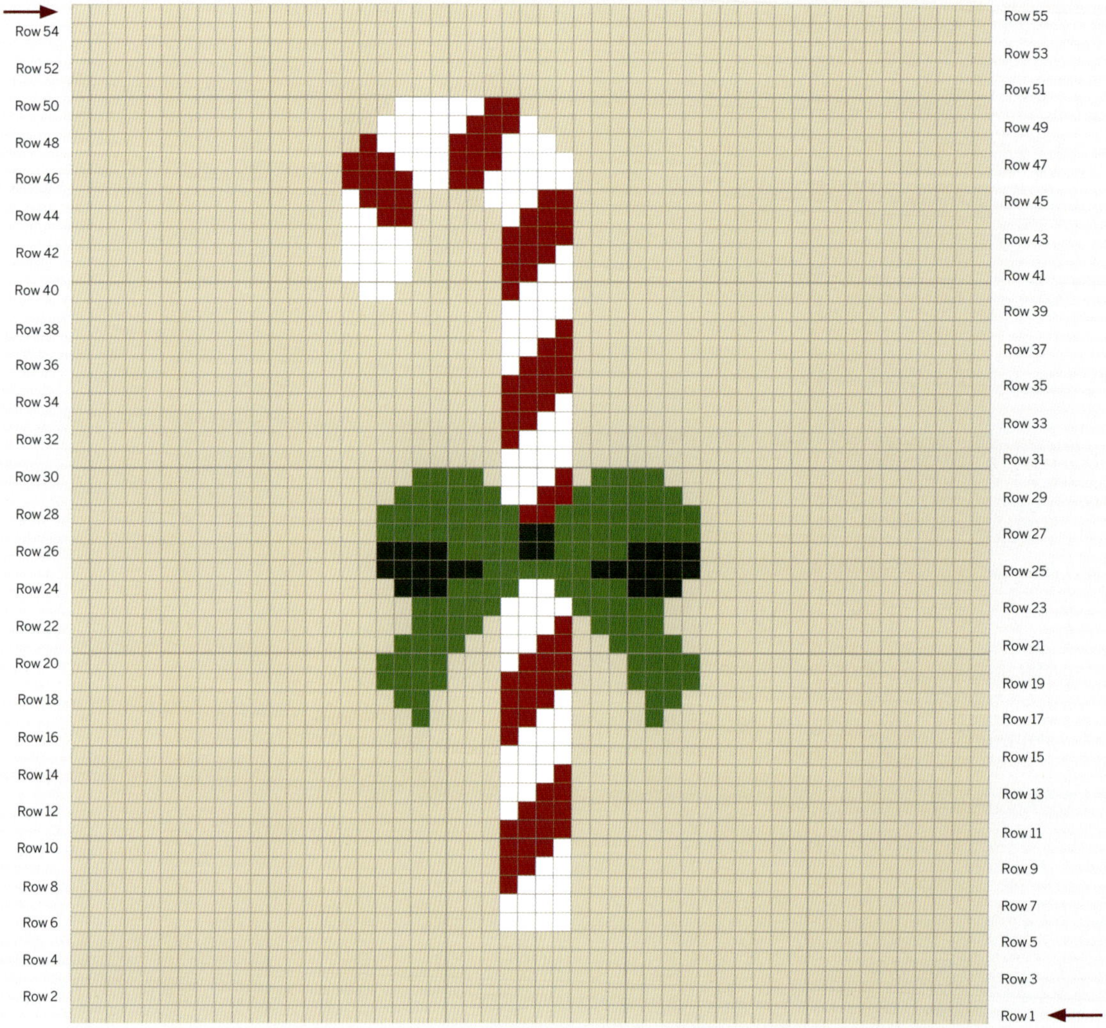

= Color 46—Sand

= Color 01—Natural White

= Color 35—Red

= Color 42—Moss Green

= Color 45—Bottle Green

← = The chart is read from right to left and crocheted on RS of work.

→ = The chart is read from left to right and crocheted on WS of work.

CHART 2—GINGERBREAD HOUSE

= Color 46—Sand
= Color 30—Brown
= Color 01—Natural White
= Color 35—Red
= Color 42—Moss Green
= Color 09—Mustard
= Color 26—Dark Blue

The gingerbread house will be easier to crochet if the small details are embroidered on with cross stitch afterward. The candy canes and door frame are instead crocheted with color 30, Brown, while the lights on the roof are crocheted with color 01, Natural White.

After finishing the crochet, embroider the detail colors with cross stitch as shown on chart.

← = The chart is read from right to left and crocheted on RS of work.

→ = The chart is read from left to right and crocheted on WS of work.

CHART 3—CHRISTMAS TREE

= Color 46—Sand
= Color 30—Brown
= Color 42—Moss Green
= Color 35—Red
= Color 09—Mustard
= Color 26—Dark Blue

The Christmas tree will be easier to crochet if the lights, red garlands, and star are embroidered on with cross stitch afterward.

After finishing the crochet, embroider the small details in colors shown on chart. If desired, use Shiny Glimmergarn to enhance the Christmas light.

← = The chart is read from right to left and crocheted on RS of work.

→ = The chart is read from left to right and crocheted on WS of work.

CHART 4—BRAIDED HEART

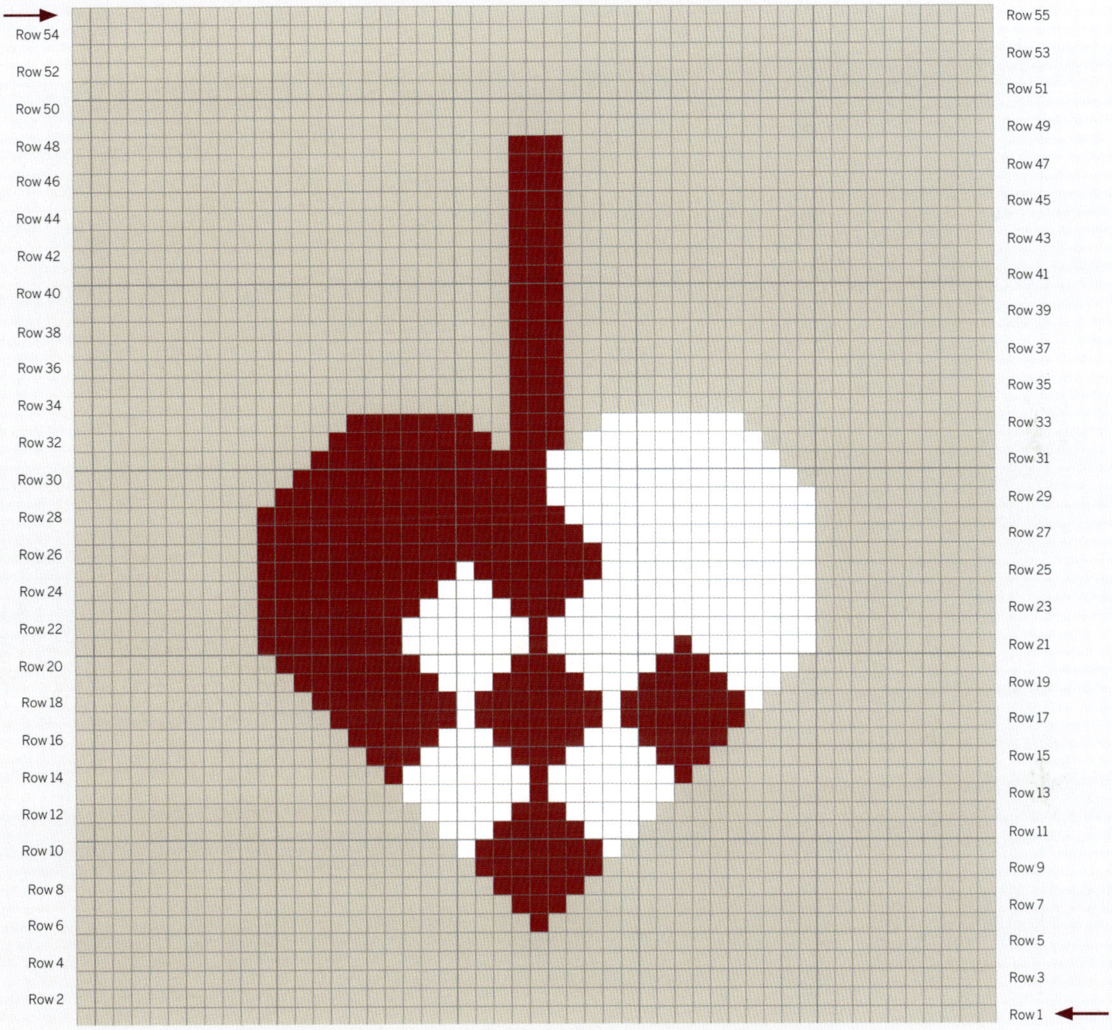

= Color 46—Sand

= Color 01—Natural White

= Color 35—Red

← = The chart is read from right to left and crocheted on RS of work.

→ = The chart is read from left to right and crocheted on WS of work.

CHART 5—CHRISTMAS GOAT

= Color 46—Sand

= Color 52—Cognac

= Color 35—Red

The Christmas goat will be easier to crochet if the whole body of the goat is crocheted with color 52, Cognac, including stitches shown in Red on the chart.

Afterward, you can embroider the bands with Red in with cross stitch.

If desired, use Shiny Glimmergarn to enhance the Christmas glow.

← = The chart is read from right to left and crocheted on RS of work.

→ = The chart is read from left to right and crocheted on WS of work.

CHART 6—DRUM

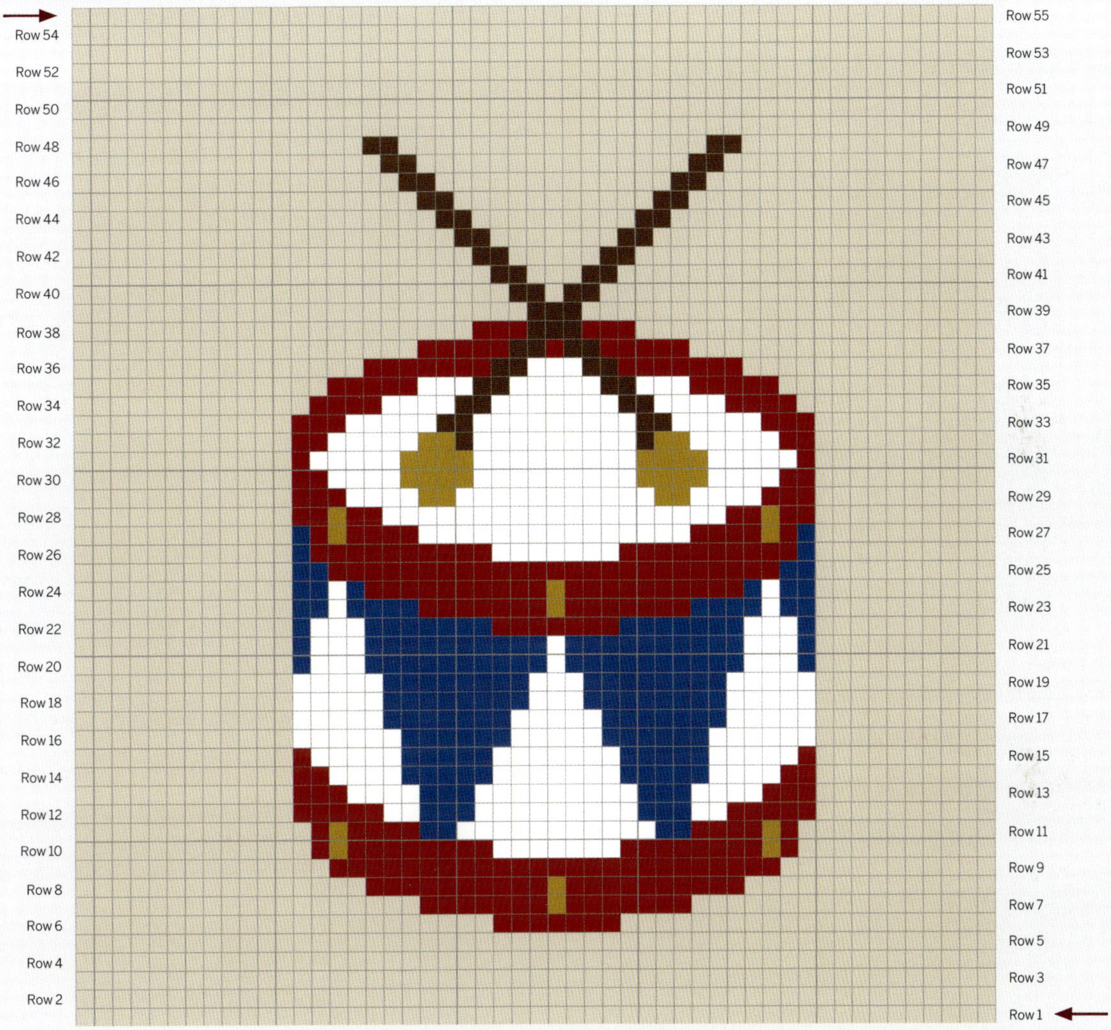

= Color 46—Sand
= Color 01—Natural White
= Color 35—Red
= Color 09—Mustard
= Color 26—Dark Blue
= Color 30—Brown

The drum will be easier to crochet if small details are embroidered on with cross stitch afterward.

On the surfaces where the drumsticks and screws on the drum are, crochet with color 01, Natural White on top of drum and color 35, Red on edges of drum.

After finishing the crochet, use cross stitch to embroider the small details in colors shown on chart.

If desired, use Shiny Glimmergarn to enhance the Christmas glow.

← = The chart is read from right to left and crocheted on RS of work.

→ = The chart is read from left to right and crocheted on WS of work.

ACKNOWLEDGMENTS

Our diligent test crocheters have always been so thorough at testing all the patterns and helping to crochet the models for photography. There are so many hours of work behind this book and we are very thankful for our fantastic network.

A thousand thank you's to Karen, Kirstine, Line, Lene, Gitte, Mathilde, Stine, Pia, Jacqueline, Julie, Kirsten, Maria, Nanna, Cecilie, Jannie, and Carina.

During the time we write books, it can be difficult to juggle between developing new patterns with set deadlines and, at the same time, carrying out the daily duties at Krea Deluxe. We offer our families special thanks for having extra patience with us, when everything notches up to a higher level.

The Woodland Lodge
In the Fredskoven at Gisselfeld, you'll find an old forest knight's residence, which has now been transformed into a fantastic hideaway. The place oozes history and has the most fantastic windows, stairs, doors, etc. We are thankful to Syska and Morten who run the place, for granting us permission to take photos for the book in their lovely locale. The place has a great deal of significance for our family because Heidi had her wedding party in the forest at the Villa Galina and overnighted at the Woodland Lodge in one of the fantastic suites and our whole family has gone on countless walks in the forest.

Gisselfeld Kloster
Christmas tree production and decorative greenery is one part of Gisselfeld Kloster's forestry business and we were given permission to choose the exact Christmas tree we wanted for the photoshoot, the one to bear all the crocheted Christmas decorations for the book. Christmas trees in June have a lot of soft, green shoots, but, luckily, we were able to take the finest Christmas tree pictures with a lovely Christmas feeling on a nice warm summer day.

Montgomery
The photographer David Bering, from the communications office Montgomery, is our steadfast photographer and he has taken photos for all of our books. We love the way David manages to bring out the best in everything, whatever we place in front of his lens, no matter whether it is the first day or the last of a 12-hour photo shoot.

Turbine Publishers
Our publisher always agrees with our book ideas and our editor, Marie, is a fantastic partner. Camilla and Karin carefully proofread, edit, and design, and we are super happy and thankful for such good collaboration with them for the book.

Sisters **Heidi B. Johannessen** and **Pia H. H. Johannesen** are the founders of Krea Deluxe, where they enjoy working together every day. Heidi and Pia create designer crochet and knitting patterns and kits, and develop Krea's line of high-quality organic yarns (GOTS-certified). Their beautifully colored yarns and designs are sold around the world. They live in Denmark.

Facebook.com/kreadeluxe
Instagram.com/kreadeluxe
www.kreadeluxe.com